Creating the Teachable Moment

An Innovative Approach to Teaching & Learning

Creating the Teachable Moment

*An Innovative
Approach to
Teaching &
Learning*

Darlene L. Stewart

Human Services Institute
Bradenton, Florida

TAB BOOKS

Blue Ridge Summit, PA

Human Services Institute publishes books on human problems, especially those affecting families and relationships: addiction, stress, alienation, violence, parenting, gender, and health. Experts in psychology, medicine, and the social sciences have gained invaluable new knowledge about prevention and treatment, but there is a need to make this information available to the public. Human Services Institute books help bridge the information gap between experts and people with problems.

FIRST EDITION
FIRST PRINTING

© 1993 by **Darlene L. Stewart**.
Published by HSI and TAB Books.
TAB Books is a division of McGraw-Hill, Inc.

Library of Congress Cataloging-in-Publication Data

Stewart, Darlene L.
    Creating the teachable moment / by Darlene L. Stewart.
        p.   cm.
    ISBN 0-8306-3089-9 (pbk.)
    1. Teaching.   2. Learning, Psychology of.   3. Stress (Psychology)
I. Title.
LB1025.3.S75   1992
371.1'02—dc20
                                                                92-23434
                                                                    CIP

Questions regarding the content of this book should be addressed to:

Human Services Institute, Inc.
P.O. Box 14610
Bradenton, FL 34280

Acquisitions Editor: Kimberly Tabor
Development Editor: Lee Marvin Joiner, Ph.D.
Copy Editor: Pat Holliday
Cover Design by Holberg Design, York, Pa.
Cover Photography by Thompson Photography, Baltimore, Md.

Dedication

To my husband, Charles, without whose support this book could not have been written.

To all my teachers and students through the years. I've been fortunate to have extraordinary ones.

To you, the reader; for whom this book was written and to whom its wisdom belongs.

Contents

| **Preface** || *Why I Wrote*
|| *This Book*

I finally learned the secret to high-powered, low-stress, success-oriented teaching and learning. It came after fifteen years of teaching, counseling and parenting experience and a series of fortunate encounters with some particularly excellent teachers.

Now I know why one moment people are bright and clear-headed and the next moment they are discouraged and dimwitted; and I know how to change it around again. Now I know what makes people friendly and cooperative one minute and grouchy and oppositional the next; and how to turn it back again. Now I know why one moment we can't see the solution to a problem, then later, the answer seems obvious. The secret is in the state of the mind.

Intelligence, clear thinking, insight and inspiring feelings of all kinds are natural by-products of the mind operating at peak condition, in positive states or good moods. Conversely, mental blocks, faulty thinking, confusion and discouraging feelings are by-products of the mind operating inefficiently, in negative states or bad moods. Thanks to recent breakthroughs in cognitive psychology, we now know: *human psychological functioning is mood-related*!

Frankly, when I first heard this theory, it had a certain ring of truth, but I was skeptical. I'd found so many sound-good theories that worked beautifully in the research lab but failed miserably in the real-world, in the classroom, office and home. But intrigued, I decided to put the mood-theory to the test, to see for myself, first-hand, if people's state of mind, influenced their moment-to-moment level of functioning. The results were surprising.

The first surprise came at home. When I was in a negative state of mind, a bad mood, my family looked helpless, dysfunctional, and impaired. Everything they did was annoying, inept or wrong. Conflicts and misunderstandings seemed unavoidable. Then, when my state of mind shifted in a positive direction, to a good mood, I felt fortunate to have such bright, extraordinary people in my life. It was a shocker.

Another shock was how my moods affected my counseling. In a good mood, I was empathic, compassionate, and inspired; I thrived on my work and wouldn't have traded jobs with anybody. But when my mood dropped, I was impatient, judgmental and discontented. No longer having fun, I dreamed of running away to a tropical island with no people and no progress reports. I'd assumed burnout was due to difficult clients or unreasonable paperwork. Now I saw it was deeper than that. The clients, the caseload, the paperwork——these things did not change appreciably from one time to another, but the way I felt about them certainly did change.

In a negative mood, everything seemed gloomy and overwhelming. I couldn't cope. But when my mood changed in a positive direction, I was on top of things again, enjoying my work. It was remarkable. Testing the mood theory as a teacher, I found the same pattern. In a positive mood I was Florence Nightingale, able to leap tall buildings in a single bound; in a bad mood, I was Attila The Hun, falling miserably over my own feet.

Moreover, I discovered that everyone, family, clients, students and coworkers, were going through the same mood-related shifts in thought, perception, feeling and behavior. In good moods, people were pillars of mental health, models of self-esteem, paradigms of well-being. In bad moods, these same people were dysfunctional, prototypes of self-depreciation, inundated with insecurity.

Previously, when I'd gotten upset, I thought it was because of what was happening out there, in the situation. Now, for the first time, I began to realize: *upsets start inside, a result of what we are thinking, perceiving and feeling in a negative state of mind!*

Then I made the most amazing discovery of all: *we can intentionally change moods.* And the instant we shift from a negative state of mind to a positive one, our thoughts, feelings, perceptions, behaviors, point of view, stress level, personality and options immediately change for the better!

A change in state of mind makes insecure people secure; angry people calm; resistant people cooperative; confused people clearheaded. These mood-related discoveries transformed my parenting, teaching and counseling practices, and brought unprecedented results.

Creating Teachable Moments was inspired by a series of insights about teaching and learning that came because of my work with moods. Two of the most important insights are:

1. Not all moments are teachable.
2. Teachable moments can be created.

Not all moments are teachable. In negative moods people lose their edge, their thoughts are cloudy, their attention is distracted and their feelings are disturbing. But——and this is the basic premise of this book——*unteachable moments can be changed to teachable ones by changing the mood.* It's easy. Anyone can do it. But there is one catch and it's a big one. So I'll tell you what it is right from the beginning.

The key to turning unteachable moments into teachable ones, the key to tapping your deepest intelligence, common sense, talents and abilities, the key to helping other people tap theirs, is *learning to live in positive, composed states of mind.* In short, to create teachable moments you have to be willing to let yourself be happy, most of the time.

Being happier more of the time means changing the way you think. You have to be willing to set aside negative, self-limiting, self-defeating thoughts, the ones that keep you stressed and discontented. You have to be willing to endure success, to get excellent, unbelievable results; and for classroom teachers this means shattering achievement test norms.

For years I walked a straight line in tight shoes, struggling to be perfect and do my best. Then, understanding that the mind works best in positive moods and breaks down in negative moods, I realized: *the secret to successful teaching and learning is not stress, it's freedom.* It's not seriousness; it's good humor. It's not tension and mean-spiritedness, believing in and expecting the worst; it's affection, generosity, and believing in and expecting the best.

Assessing and modifying moods is the secret to creating teachable moments. Stress, fear and insecurity impair mental processes. Optimism, boldness and enjoyment open thought. Superior teachers who love what they're doing, challenge, encourage, support and inspire excellence. Love opens minds. You can't love in a low-mood state of mind. You can't even like.

This book has one goal: I want to show you how to be a splendid, happy, stress-free teacher and learner. I want to show you how to live in the higher levels of consciousness so you tap directly into your deepest intelligence, your wisdom, your clearest, insightful thinking, and teach other people to do the same.

This book presents four principles of psychological functioning based on the most recent, cream-of-the-crop discoveries in cognitive psychology; discoveries that shed new light on intelligence, thinking, feelings and behavior. When you understand these principles you find excellent answers to everyday problems within yourself——by tapping your innate potential for common sense, insight and creativity.

The primary subject of this book is to teach you to create teachable moments. The underlying subjects are commitment, discipline, craftsmanship, the need for us to learn to live together joyfully, to honor one another and to know how to do that. It's about the personal rewards of being in control of your life, in finding your power——your own unique voice.

This scientific, principle-based psychology and philosophy of teaching strengthens any interaction, activity, learning style or teaching method. It can be used beautifully anytime, anywhere, in the kitchen, living room, classroom or office. This approach upgrades teaching effectiveness across the board, for all people, in all settings, at all levels, regardless of age, sex, IQ, cultural background or experience.

Teachable moments don't cost money or take special equipment. There's nothing to memorize. The only requirement is understanding certain principles of psychological functioning that enable you to live your best and bring out the best in others. This approach is so simple, so solid, so practical and so effective you will use it everyday of your life with wonderful results.

Sometimes we get so discouraged. We've worked so hard for so long we lose hope and think it can't be any other way. But we didn't start out that way. We started out with a beautiful dream, believing all good things were possible. But we got lost because we didn't know that thought creates drudgery just as easily as it creates wonder. But now we know, and that knowledge makes all the difference in the world.

If you want to create wonderfully teachable moments and avoid the drudgery of unteachable ones, if you want a success-oriented approach to teaching and learning that is effective, productive and downright satisfying, if you want consistently superior, accelerated results without strain or without fear or failure, this book was written for you.

This book, based on more than thirty-five years of experience, is full of interesting, real-life stories of people who created teachable moments by working with, rather than against, the functioning of the mind. Reading this book, you will know in a few weeks what it's taken me these thirty-five years to learn. That's the way it should be. Later, when you write a book sharing what you've learned, and you see the people reading it leapfrogging ahead of you, you'll be glad. That's the way teaching works.

D.S.

Getting Started

How Will This Book Help Me?

1

What are

Teachable Moments?

In teachable moments, connected to our bigger mind and larger self, we are open like we were at first, before we learned to believe that learning, loving, growing and changing were hard.

Some moments are magic. Thought is clear. You feel alive, connected, in-sync, so absorbed in what you are doing that you lose track of time. Mental fog evaporates, vision expands, creativity sparks and imaginative juices flow. Without thinking about it, you know just what to do to get excellent results. You have a sense of humor, see the lighter side of life and feel optimistic about the future. Other peoples' responses to you are friendly and cooperative.

These are teachable moments. Whether they happen alone or with others, teachable moments are powerful and memorable. Unfortunately, not all moments are teachable.

Some moments are drudgery. Thought is muddled and cumbersome. Everything looks glum; you feel dumpy, unmotivated, out-of-sync, stuck. Everything seems difficult. You vacillate, hesitate, wobble. No matter what you do, it isn't quite right. Other people get on your nerves; they're in your way. You feel like you're drinking the swimming pool just to keep from drowning. These are unteachable moments.

Cognitive psychology has made a ground-breaking discovery: there is a direct connection between state of mind and performance. Unteachable moments are by-products of negative states of mind or bad moods. Teachable moments are by-products of positive states of mind or good mood. A mood is more than passing emotional weather——it is a level of psychological functioning! In good moods, our functioning is high. In bad moods, our functioning is impaired. Who would have guessed? Our state of mind affects the learning curve!

The optimal psychological condition for inspired teaching is a positive state of mind. A teachable moment occurs when a teacher in a positive state of mind interacts with learners who are in positive states of mind. When teachers are in the mood to teach and learners are in the mood to learn, incredible power, genius and magic is released. People listen with a hearing that goes beyond words and see with a vision that goes beyond sight.

To create peak learning experiences consistently, to do their finest all the time——not just now and then——people must learn to tap positive states of mind. This book tells you how. A positive state of mind is not a silly, superficial, put-on-a-smiley-face attitude. It is much deeper than that. A positive state of mind is a solid feeling of security and well-being grounded in wisdom.

Understanding the principles in this book, you will bring your most affirming, doing-my-best-and-enjoying-it states of mind to any moment. You won't do it haphazardly; you will do it intentionally, knowing exactly what you're doing. You will live out of the highest of your ability not by chance, but because you planned it that way! And once your own creative state of mind is in place, you will see how to ease other people out of closed states of mind into open ones.

Creating Teachable Moments is based on the premise that the most natural state of the human being is one of security, emotional well-being, self-esteem and happiness. These qualities are all naturally present in positive states of mind. Another quality innate to positive states of mind is the deeper intelligence we call common sense and wisdom. In composed states of mind, joy, mental health, self-confidence, well-being and good judgment are givens——ours for the taking——as available as the air we breathe.

Creating Teachable Moments is a powerful, user-friendly, stress-free, approach to teaching and learning that deepens the way people listen, learn, know, grow and change. This approach, based on the premise that everything we need to be happy, healthy, successful teachers and learners is already resident within us in positive states of mind, is founded on four principles that can be learned easily and taught to others.

WHAT IS A TEACHABLE MOMENT?

Teachable moments are simple, natural moments when learned insecurities subside and the deeper, knowledgeable part of us emerges. In these moments, connected to our bigger mind and larger self, we are open like we were at first, before we learned to believe that learning, loving, growing and changing were hard.

In teachable moments you share something you care about with someone you care about. Driving down the street with your wide-awake two-year-old, seeing everything new through her eyes, you point out all the wonderful things you want her to see. "Look! There's a cow, and over there, a fire truck. Wow! Look at that bridge." The secret to successful learning is positive feeling.

Marilyn dreaded the staff meeting on Monday morning. Everybody dragged in, not wanting to face the same problems they'd struggled with for weeks. Marilyn looked at the dull, listless group and thought, "Unless we change states of mind, unless we all find a better feeling, this meeting will be a waste of time. When it's over we'll feel drained, but we won't have accomplished our goals."

Willing herself into a more optimistic state of mind, Marilyn said, "Well folks, I know you'd rather have a root canal than be here this morning, but it's my birthday so you'd better lighten-up." Instantly, people changed emotional gears. They perked up. Life came into their faces. Their eyes lit up. Smiles replaced scowls and the room filled with energy, laughter and song. After a few minutes of merrymaking, the group, still in their enlightened mood, settled down and accomplished more in one hour than they'd previously accomplished in ten.

Marilyn, a mood-wise administrator, spotted an unteachable moment and turned it into a teachable one. She did it by modifying the mood. A state of mind makes all the difference. Not all moments are created equal.

Not All Moments are Created Equal

Every person has important things to teach. Your well-being and that of your youngsters, students or clients depend on your ability to teach well, in ways that suit you. Any significant improvement in our lives or in the world, comes from our ability to teach and learn effectively from one another.

Parents are their child's first, most important teachers. Teaching all the time, we never know where our influence begins or ends. We off-handedly say something that triggers an insight that changes a person's life, and we never know it. Without giving it a thought, we offer a kind word that gives someone the strength to make it through the day, or we unthinkingly say something that wipes out someone's dignity and hope. What we teach changes the world. Creating teachable moments, we use the power of our minds to build up rather than tear down, to care rather than judge, to heal rather than hurt. It's an enormous power.

Before I knew how states of mind affected the teaching and learning process, I believed all moments were created equal. As a wife and mother, I thought if I had something to tell my family, one moment was as good as another. As a counselor, I assumed that when a client showed up for an appointment I was psychologically ready to help and they were psychologically ready to hear what I had to say. As an educator, I assumed when the bell rang I was ready to teach and the students were ready to learn. I was mistaken.

Working under this misconception, my results were just what you'd expect; within the norm. Sometimes people learned and sometimes they didn't, and I didn't know what made the difference. This changed dramatically when I started assessing moods and taking time to change unteachable moods to teachable ones.

As a classroom teacher creating teachable moments, I've seen failing, turned-off, I-won't-do-it-you-can't-make-me students, high-risk kids with learning disabilities of every kind, kids with sagging self-esteem and no hope at all, turn around and score three times higher than the norm on achievement tests. And, in the process, these kids came to life; they loved learning; they redefined who they were and what was possible for them.

As a counselor creating teachable moments, I helped clients move from insecure, confused states of mind to more stable, open states where their thinking cleared and brought feelings of mental health, self-esteem and well-being. As a wife and mother, I learned to live more consistently in states of mind that produced affection, patience, good humor and kindness. My family, grateful for the change, responded in kind. Our home, always a place we liked to be, turned into a loving, happy, peaceful place. The rewards of paying attention to states of mind were tremendous.

Anyone can create teachable moments. Once you understand the principles, it's easy. People of all ages, ability levels and all walks of life do it. A counselor in St. Louis working with severely emotionally disturbed adolescents said, "Creating teachable moments was so easy I was worried. Everything changed for the better but I didn't think I was doing anything." This is the feeling of successful teaching, counseling, parenting, loving or living. When it gets to be drudgery, we've lost our positive state of mind, and with it our optimism. In touch with optimism, life isn't a struggle, it's a dance.

PRINCIPLES FOR CREATING TEACHABLE MOMENTS

Creating teachable moments is made easy by following four basic principles of human psychological functioning. These principles are important educational guidelines because they hold consistent predictive power across all variations of age, sex, IQ, culture or experience. They apply to all facets of learning: motivation, achievement and productivity. And they apply any time, any place, in all settings and circumstances.

The principles for creating teachable moments are an outgrowth of the ideas first presented in the book, *Sanity, Insanity and Common Sense*, which I coauthored with Rick Suarez and Roger Mills.[1] Those ideas sparked the insights presented in this book. The principles for creating teachable moments are, in brief, as follows.

PRINCIPLE I: INTELLIGENCE IS MULTIDIMENSIONAL.

In addition to IQ, the acquired storehouse of information, every human is born with a profound natural intelligence. This deeper dimension of intelligence, often called wisdom, is the source of common sense, good judgment, instinct, intuition, hunches and insight. Wisdom is more universal and objective than personal thought. It is our great pool of awareness about life that enables us to learn, grow, change and evolve.

Because of multidimensional intelligence, learning is a process of realizing something we already know. We cannot learn something that is not already a part of our consciousness. You say to a child, "When you relax, it is easier to thread the needle," and he responds, "Oh, yeah!" because on some level, he already knew that. Our task as teachers is not to force learners to realize something foreign and incomprehensible, but to help them uncover what, at a deeper level, they already know.

Because intelligence is multidimensional, we never give up on a person's ability for joyful, successful learning. Regardless of an individual's IQ, age, sex, nationality or cultural background, regardless of her present level of functioning or her experience in the past, we never stop expecting miracles.

PRINCIPLE II: INTELLIGENCE IS EXPRESSED OR SUPPRESSED BY THE WAY WE THINK.

Human beings are born with a great power. We think. We produce thought to suit ourselves. Now, on the brink of the 21st century, we make a discovery that turns our teaching and learning practices inside out: *what we think opens or closes the door to our deeper potential*. If we want to be smarter, happier, and more effective, we must start paying attention to what we think.

PRINCIPLE III: STATES OF MIND (MOODS) ARE LEVELS OF PSYCHOLOGICAL FUNCTIONING.

This principle is the working foundation of creating teachable moments. We've been aware of moods out of the corner of our eye, but we haven't really grasped what they are and the tremendous influence they exert on our moment-to-moment experience.

Mood affects what we think, what we perceive, what we feel and how we behave. Moods affects our stress level, our performance, our mental health, self-esteem and well-being. Moods affect our ability to teach and learn.

In positive states of mind we are at our best. Thought is clear, focused, in touch with our most enabling beliefs. Open to our deeper intelligence, we see possibilities, challenges, adventures. We feel ready-to-go, on top of things, hopeful in spite of the circumstances. Teaching is a pleasure and learning is a joy. But when a negative state of mind moves in, like a black cloud covering the sun, everything changes.

In negative states of mind we become functionally impaired. Thought is muddled, unfocused, weighed down by our most self-limiting beliefs. Our deeper intelligence blocked, all we see are obstacles, difficulties, and trials. We feel stuck, overwhelmed, hopeless, and without options even in the best of circumstances. In negative states of mind, teaching is drudgery and learning is fog.

To become superior, happy teachers and learners, we must start paying attention to the states of our minds. This brings us to the last principle.

PRINCIPLE IV: FEELINGS TELL WHETHER A STATE OF MIND IS POSITIVE OR NEGATIVE.

Feelings are psychological dipsticks. They let us know when we're a quart low.

Composed, optimistic feelings are signs of positive states of mind. They say, "Functioning is high. Thought is clear. Proceed and enjoy." Dense, nerve-wracking feelings are sure signs of negative states of mind. They warn, "Functioning impaired. Thought confused. Beware. Proceed with caution." Feelings tell us with unerring accuracy whether the moment is teachable or unteachable. Knowing whether the moment is teachable or not keeps you from running into walls you don't know are there.

This is an overview of the principles you need to know to create teachable moments. Following chapters elaborate on these ideas and explain their significance in more detail.

WHAT A PRINCIPLE-BASED APPROACH DOES AND DOES NOT DO

This approach does not give exact, step-by-step techniques for what to do when your child is watching *Gilligan's Island* instead of doing his homework. Exacting, first-do-this-then-do-that, techniques can't work all the time because every situation is unique, different from every other one. This approach does tell you how to go to the place inside where your good ideas come from. Then you know what to do or say, your own way, the way best suited to you and your child.

This approach doesn't tell you what to do when you are lecturing on The History Of Dirt and all eyes glaze over. It does tell you how to tap your own creative ideas for gaining the group's attention. This approach doesn't tell you what to say when a client fends off everything with, "Yes, but . . . ," or "I tried that and it doesn't work." This approach does tell you how to create states of mind where your message hits home.

Three features make creating teachable moments unique:

1. It recognizes a deeper, more profound intelligence than IQ, that is available to everyone, whatever age, sex, IQ, cultural background or experience.
2. It recognizes two separate and distinct dimensions of thought: thought content and the ability to produce, evaluate or process thought content.

3. It prepares the mind for the ultimate learning experience, the incomparably joyous, Aha!-I-see-it-now! experience of insight.

GETTING THE MOST FROM THIS BOOK

To get the most from this book, create teachable moments for yourself as you read. Read in a good mood. Get comfortable, sit in your favorite chair, drink your favorite tea from your best china cup. Clear your mind, open your thought and read with interest and curiosity, like you read a good story. Don't force it. If you force learning, ideas only stick to your short term memory, then dissolve like all the information you crammed for tests and forgot immediately afterwards. In relaxed, open, receptive states of mind, your deepest intelligence is most active.

Reading in this attitude sparks insights. Your insights are your teacher, your understanding, what will enable you to create peak teaching and learning experiences. Later, if you read the book again, beginning with a deeper understanding, you will have even more insights the second time around.

In reading this book you'll learn:

1. To live at the top, from the best of your capability
2. To recognize unteachable moments and change them to teachable ones
3. To prepare your mind, on the spot, for superior, inspired teaching
4. To prepare your listener's mind, on the spot, for peak learning
5. To maintain your sanity until teachable moments appear
6. To recognize and build on the innate worth, and strength of yourself and others

SUMMARY

Life is a series of moments, of constantly changing, ebbing and flowing states of minds. Each mood affects, for good or ill, our ability to teach and learn brilliantly, joyfully. In positive moods, feeling connected, awake and engaged, teachable moments arise. In negative states of mind—feeling disconnected, sleepy, closed and distracted—unteachable moments dominate.

When we teach oblivious to states of mind, we miss opportunities and possibilities we never knew existed. When we teach taking states of mind in account, we intentionally create the space where magic happens.

2 Chico Learns to Read

In positive states of mind a teacher is in the mood to teach and students are in the mood to learn.

The first time I met Chico at the educational clinic, his brown eyes brimmed with tears; "I can't read," he said. "I've never been able to do it. There's something wrong with me. I've got a learning disability." Trembling visibly, Chico was the most frightened student I'd ever met.

Chico, a seventh grader reading on a first grade level, had years of classroom defeat behind him. He felt damaged, cheated at birth out of some basic ability that everyone else seemed to have. Chico felt powerless to do what he wanted to do, what his family and teachers wanted him to do: to be a good student. To save face, Chico feigned an I-don't-care-about-learning-reading-is-beneath-me attitude.

I asked, "Chico, how many languages do you know?" He answered, "Two, Spanish and English." "That's interesting. You are fluent in two languages that you learned as baby but you think you can't learn to read. Tell me something. When you meet people—before they say a word—you know whether to speak to them in English or Spanish. Am I right?" Puzzled, Chico admitted, "Yeah. That's right."

I remembered getting on an elevator with a Cuban boy, about five years old, who was chattering in lively Spanish with his grandmother. In the middle of his talk, he looked at me, sized me up in an instant, and in perfect English asked, "What floor do you want, ma'am?" This boy, like Chico, took for granted the difficult, abstract learning he'd mastered.

I said to Chico, "Anyone who has learned two languages can learn to read. Easily. You've had some bad experiences in school and now that's all you think about. But keeping your mind full of past failures only clogs your thoughts so your intelligence can't come through. Forget the past. Get interested in what's happening now and I guarantee your mind will open. You will learn and it will be easy. Pay attention, practice, enjoy your success and pretty soon you'll be a reading superstar, slam-dunking words like Michael Jordan slam-dunks basketballs." Chico was skeptical. His previous experience with reading taught him one thing: reading was hard and he couldn't do it.

Chico was right in one way and wrong in another. He was correct in thinking I couldn't teach him to read. Reading, like walking, is far too complex for one person to teach it to another without cooperation, maturation, and a wealth of supporting experiences. But, he was wrong to think he couldn't learn to read. When Chico felt safe, when he relaxed and forgot he couldn't read, his thought would open, his natural intelligence would spill into it and he would learn to read just like he learned to talk and operate the VCR.

Working with Chico, I proceeded on the following assumptions:

- People want to learn, even when they adopt an I-don't-care attitude.
- Learning to read is easy and satisfying.
- A successful learner associates learning with success.
- In positive states of mind, thought is an open channel to our deepest intelligence.
- In negative states of mind, the natural flow of intelligence is blocked.

To create teachable moments, I worked a four-point plan:

1. Keep the mood positive.
2. Build a friendly, supportive, cooperative, relationship.

3. Ensure success.
4. Trust Chico's ability to learn through insight.

KEEPING THE MOOD POSITIVE

The teacher's mood sets the tone of the class. A teacher in a negative state of mind—an impatient or agitated mood—sets a negative classroom atmosphere which arouses negative thoughts, feelings, perceptions and behaviors. To create an environment that bring out people's best learning potential, a teacher must be in a composed state of mind, a good mood. This point is essential, the key to all the rest. In positive states of mind a teacher is in the mood to teach and to create a classroom atmosphere in which students are ready to learn.

Through my mood I made the classroom an interesting, friendly place where students wanted to be; a place where they felt respected, safe from ridicule or failure; a place where they could laugh and enjoy themselves; a place where they could learn to think differently about learning and what was possible for them.

To keep my state of mind positive, I took an active interest in my own enjoyment. I planned lessons I liked to teach. I did things I liked to do. If something wasn't interesting to me, I changed it so it was. If I proposed something Chico didn't like, we might negotiate in good humor until we found common ground. Other times I'd say, "This is non-negotiable. Do it because it will make you an excellent reader. When you're finished, we'll do something you choose." It was fun, always interesting, to step into a world of Chico's choosing.

If either Chico or I were in an impatient or distracted state of mind, I didn't try to teach, but took that as a signal to tend to the mood. We'd stop and play a reading game, do a crossword puzzle, read classic comics, or look up the story of the Loch Ness monster in the encyclopedia—something Chico never tired of doing. After a few minutes, the mood would change and we'd continue our original activity. When Chico came to class sick, exhausted or in a I-won't-do-it-you-can't-make-me mood that he wouldn't change, as he sometimes did, it was impossible to teach so I'd read him a story. He'd settle down and leave class in a better mood, but it meant we had a period with no formal instruction. I worried about missing instruction time, but I knew keeping the mood positive was essential, not only to successful teaching, but to building the constructive relationship on which productive teaching is based.

The success or failure of teaching hinges on the relationship between teacher and student. To create the most constructive relationship possible, I became interested in Chico as a person. I made it a point to enjoy his company and let him know it. I found out what he liked to do after school and on weekends, the color of his bike and where he liked to ride it, what pets he had, what their names were and what funny things they did. I knew his favorite music and television programs, the names of his best friends and if he had a girlfriend this week. I discovered what helped him relax and what made him laugh. I found out he loved green Life Saver candies, so I stocked up on them.

When people sincerely like and respect one another, the relationship brings out the best in both of them. Genuinely liking Chico, keying on his best qualities——his strengths and his interests——helped me to motivate, encourage and support him. It made me more compassionate and responsive to his needs and preferences. Since Chico liked and respected me, he worked hard and was willing to take a risk when I asked him to do something difficult. Maintaining a positive relationship contributed to our success as a team.

To be a successful reader, Chico had to associate reading with success. I wanted Chico to learn without being penalized for making mistakes. When he made an error and groaned in remorse, I said, "Good eye! You noticed that." When he stumbled on words and sighed in mortification, I'd say, "You are doing better today than you did yesterday," or, "You have the determination of a samurai warrior," or "I've never seen anybody try as hard as you do." This was not insincerity or false cheerfulness. When my attitude was in the right place I could appreciate Chico's efforts and I simply told him in all honesty what I saw.

In a positive state of mind I maintained discipline with firmness and good humor. This was important. Badger or intimidate a struggling reader and he becomes a worse reader. I wanted our relationship to enhance, not detract from Chico's natural ability to learn.

When Chico's mind was free of self-limiting thoughts and self-induced fear (two by-products of negative states of mind), he was capable of learning, just the way he learned two languages as a baby. Trusting that gave me the courage to proceed with confidence, to work easy, to back off when something wasn't working. I didn't have to make Chico a reader; all I had to do was create the state of mind in which Chico could rise above his self-defeating cognition. Then he would make himself a reader.

WORKING THE PLAN

I taught reading the usual ways with one exception. I paid strict attention to mood, keeping Chico's morale up and his spirits high. I searched out good, interesting stories at Chico's ability level and made reading pleasant and challenging, but not overwhelming. When Chico got stuck on a word, I used my judgment. Sometimes I supplied words so he wouldn't get bogged down and lose track of the story; other times I offered clues; and then there were times when it seemed important for him to come to terms with words in his own way.

After reading the story, we'd talk about it, what we liked, what we didn't like, which characters we identified with, what would happen if we changed a key event and so on. I'd try to stump him on obscure details and he'd make fun of my perversity. We discussed, joked and laughed and devoured packages of green Life Saver candies.

A BREAKTHROUGH

The first week I introduced a simple vocabulary game. I'd hold up a card with a word on it. If Chico said the word correctly, he got a point; if not, I'd get it. When I proposed the game, Chico's face turned white. Paralyzed by fear, his brain wouldn't work. He blanked on the first four words, so I gave enormous, funny clues and awarded him the point. Still, he was scared to death.

I held up the next card. He looked at it, turned white and said, "Oh, God." I got a silly look on my face and said, "Boy, you must really be scared if you have to say a prayer before you can read a word." Chico looked at me blankly for a second, and I said, "A joke, Chico; that was a joke. For heaven's sake man, lighten up." He smiled and said, "Only you could find something funny about reading." Then I held up the next card, R-O-S-E. He froze. Grasping at straws he blurted out, "Car."

I turned the card over and looked at it. Feigning astonishment, I said, "R-O-S-E. Car? Car? You've got to be kidding. The word begins with 'R' for Pete's sake. If you're going to guess, you could at least guess an 'R' word like row or rowdy or reckless or ragamuffin. R-O-S-E. Car? Give me a break here."

Chico stared at me for a second, then began to laugh. The longer he laughed, the funnier it got. "R-o-s-e. CAR," he said, hugging his sides with both hands. "That's funny." He tried to compose himself. I held up the next card, "Now remember, if the world begins with R, you can say Ralph, Rumpelstiltskin, rip-roaring or rump, but please, whatever you do, don't say CAR." It was too much. Chico started laughing again and this time he couldn't stop. He fell off his chair and rolled on the floor holding himself. He'd pull himself together, get back on the chair, look at me and start laughing again. For twenty minutes Chico laughed. When people from other classes looked in to see what going on, it only made him laugh more. Tears rolled down his face. His shut-in, scared place was opening; Chico looked into the face of the enemy and saw it was a joke. After that, he looked forward to class. He enjoyed reading so much he didn't notice the days flying by.

One day, with the tropical summer Florida rain pouring down outside, I said, "Chico, it's time for the posttest." He froze. "Please don't ask me to take the test," he begged. "I'll die." Taking care of the mood, I said, "Don't worry Chico. I haven't yet lost a student to Death-By-Testing." He groaned at the weak joke but smiled in spite of himself. We joked back and forth for a few minutes, stared at the rain, munched Life Saver candies, then he said, "I'm ready." Like a great warrior with green lips, Chico faced the firing squad.

The next day I had his test corrected. Just seeing it in my hand took Chico's breath away. He said, "Oh, no. Not that thing." I said, "If you promise to breathe, I have some good news." He swallowed, took a deep breath, a handful of Life Saver candies and braced himself for the worst. I said, "Chico, eight weeks ago on the pretest you were reading on a first grade level." His face flushed with shame. I continued, "Now, on this test, the one you took yesterday, you are reading well into the sixth grade level. Do you know what this means?" He stared at me mute, open-mouthed, uncomprehending. "It means you learned five years of reading in eight weeks. He blinked. I continued, "Just think of the intelligence you have to have to be able to do that. Learning five years of reading in eight weeks isn't something a learning disabled person could do. You've come a long way from 'R-O-S-E,' 'CAR.'"

Chico hung in midair, suspended in disbelief. I repeated his success again and again, giving him time for the meaning of it to sink in. He was stunned, shaken, fragile, reborn, not yet knowing this new person in his skin. He left class that day in a daze. He didn't even say goodbye. Moments later he was back. He looked at me, again his brown eyes brimming with tears and said, "I can read. I really can read. There's nothing wrong with me after all!"

SUMMARY

Birds fly. Fish swim. And, in positive states of mind with their most constructive thoughts, perceptions, feelings and behaviors in place, people learn. Sometimes they learn spectacularly, like Chico, other times their gains are more modest. In positive states of mind, all you have to do is be there when knowledge appears.

To be there when knowledge appears, to be part of this great, wonderful, mysterious, experience, either as a teacher or a learner, is one of life's truly great satisfactions.

3

Putting Teachable Moments

to the Test

The mind ready to learn is an unstoppable force.

Preparing minds for teaching and learning seems like an obvious thing to do; just good common sense. But it's only recently, in the last few years, that we've realized that our state of mind at the moment has a profound effect on the level of our performance. As a new teacher just starting out, I had no idea that my state of mind was so important.

A NEW TEACHER HITS THE WALL

I couldn't wait to be a teacher, to do good work and make a difference. I was in the classroom early the first day of school. The warm September sun poured through the big windows and spilled in bright patches on the small wooden desks. As the first graders arrived, they looked sweet and adorable and I thought, "This is going to be a great year. I will touch these young minds and make them strong and good and happy. And they will love me."

But those adorable kids had other plans. They didn't want to sit. They didn't want to listen. They wanted to talk and giggle and horse around. They wanted to make paper airplanes out of the papers I'd stayed up half the night to prepare. They wanted to wipe their noses on their workbook pages and make obscene noises with their armpits. They wanted to vomit on my shoes. They wanted to kill me.

These helter-skelter, rambunctious, everywhere-all-at-once-like-fleas-on-a-dog kids were more interested in eating crayons, peeing their pants and hiding their soggy underwear in the gerbil cage than in delving into the masterwork, *See Dick Run*.

We made tulips. Theirs were wild, madcap, multicolored hues and shades of all sizes and shapes. Where, I wondered, were the well-ordered, all-in-a-row, every-one-looking-exactly-like-every-other-one tulips my teachers had cherished. This wasn't what I remembered. Those wild things hammered through my nervous system like a hurricane pounds the suburbs. Like the temperature in July, my stress level soared.

Thwarted, I talked faster. But the faster I talked the more disinterested they became. I talked louder. But the louder I got, the more their volume increased. I tried behavior modification. "I like the way Susie is listening," but I felt silly saying it and everyone, except Susie, was unimpressed hearing it.

Struggling against the robust energy of twenty-seven six-year-olds wore me out. I lost my positive mood, my sense of humor and common sense. I yelled for quiet. I disrespectfully demanded respect. I swatted students for hitting other people. I rudely corrected impolite behavior. I scolded, lectured, pontificated and moralized, but like a gnat flying against a high wind, I made little headway. Before the big orange pumpkins hit the October bulletin boards, I was drained, mean-spirited, pathetic.

Fear at my back, trying too hard to be perfect and get everything done just right, I was afraid to relax, to put my feet up, to let my hair down, to have fun, to go with the flow. The life went out of me and my teaching. A tense, anxious mood became a lifestyle. It wasn't always this way.

As a youngster, I was filled with hope, spirit and imagination, but I put on adulthood like a coat of armor. I put my wacky humor, my delight in silliness for silliness sake and my great love of laughter on the shelf and only brought them out for picnics or Friday-at-Five. As a teacher, I became stodgy, finicky and brittle yet I couldn't understand why the kids weren't interested in what I had to say.

Trying desperately to pack in all the requirements, I started teaching the minute the bell rang at eight-fifteen and didn't stop until the dismissal bell rang six hours later, when the word-worn students made their escape in abject relief. "Don't tell me the guppy died or that the first snow flakes of winter are falling outside our window. Don't tell me you didn't have breakfast or that you're scared by your parent's fighting. I don't have time. It's not on the plan. We study fish in the spring, our weather and nutrition units are six weeks away and your family life class comes the second semester of your sophomore year."

Something was wrong but I didn't know what it was. I was teaching as I'd been taught to teach, but it wasn't working. Deciding I wasn't cut out to be a teacher, I went back to school and became a counselor. But still not realizing the importance of state of mind, I'd get into oppositional postures with clients and they'd shut me out.

Then, oh, happy day, I discovered that when I kept my state of mind open, allied, we're-in-this-together, on-the-same-side, people responded in kind and the moment was teachable. This approach brought beautiful results at home and in counseling sessions, but how, I wondered, would it work in the classroom? To find out, I became a teacher in an educational clinic.

A NEW APPROACH TO TEACHING

This time I knew what I didn't know before——the importance of maintaining a positive state of mind. If the teacher isn't in the mood to teach or the students aren't in the mood to learn, you can push, you can nag, you can go, robot-like, through the motions of teaching while your students go robot-like through the motions of listening, but it's a waste of time. The kids who always get "A"'s will still get "A"'s, and the kids who always get "D"'s will still get "D"'s but in either case nothing real and vital and alive has happened. Teaching devoid of vitality, creativity and fun is only a simulated educational experience. There's no life in it. No magic. No wonder, surprise or delight for the teacher or the student. Blah. Boring. Is it Friday, yet?

This time around, I wanted teaching to be different. My plan was to teach reading the usual ways, with one exception; I would not begin instruction until I was in the mood to teach and the student was in the mood to learn.

GETTING THE TEACHER IN THE MOOD TO TEACH

This time, knowing that a cooperative, good-humored state of mind was my greatest teaching resource, I took utmost care to safeguard my good mood. If I came to class distracted, agitated or disinterested, I didn't try to teach until I'd shaken off the blahs and felt glad to be there, ready, willing and able to begin.

Usually, just realizing that I was in a bad mood, an impaired level of functioning that would spread through the class like a virulent virus, was enough to snap me out of it. If it wasn't, if I needed more time, I'd engage the students in conversation, play a game or read a story aloud. Maybe I'd assign silent reading while I took a deep breath and looked out the window, walked down the hall for a drink of water or did paperwork. Sometimes I felt better having a snack or a cup of coffee. I deliberately threw myself into anything I could think of that would help me disengage from the negative thinking that was keeping my unproductive mood alive.

When my mood was composed and my attention was fully in the room, I was interested, creative, responsive, helpful. Now I could discipline without destruction. Now I could state facts objectively, without rancor, "If you aren't going to listen you'll have to leave the classroom," and follow through with kind firmness without losing my sanity or damaging a student's self-esteem.

In a raw mood, I wasted energy on battles that could be avoided, quarrels that could be quelled. My time and talent were squandered on useless conflicts which I kept going. "What's wrong with you? I don't have all day. Why do you *always* not listen? Why do you *never* pay attention? Are you naturally slow or is someone helping you?" This tirade provided an already-inattentive student with even more prosaic images to envision. Now he could imagine his teacher being eaten alive by fire ants.

A teacher's mood infects the class. Mean moods propagate meanness. Distracted moods disseminate distraction. Blah moods beget boredom. Composed moods create composure. Interested moods invite interest. My new teaching plan was to be in a coonstructive teaching mood so I could guide students into a constructive learning mood.

GETTING THE STUDENTS IN THE MOOD TO LEARN

The students in this clinic would rather have their teeth pulled than read. They'd given up long ago. Their resignation to failure was evident in their beaten-down moods. Some were sullen and lethargic, others were agitated or scared. Some covered up their failure with an I-don't-care, reading-is-beneath-me attitude. To change these anti-learning moods to pro-learning moods, I'd start non-threateningly with friendly conversation. Then, when the feeling was less guarded, I'd say, "Reading is not only easy, it's fun. I'll show you. I'm on your side. We're a team. I'll do everything I can to help you succeed." Students were skeptical but intrigued. When they left the first day of class, their no-hope moods had already been disturbed, poked by tiny rays of hope.

Every day, I'd start out establishing a cooperative, I-think-I-can-do-it attitude, then we'd begin reading. I choose interesting, easy, no-fail material so students would feel the greatest mood-builder of all time: success. As their confidence grew, they handled increasingly difficult material. Any time the feeling changed (mine or theirs) from cooperation to resistance, we'd stop and talk or stretch or play a game until the good feeling returned, then we'd proceed refreshed.

Through the thin partitions that separated one room from another, I could hear the other teachers struggling against the flow of negative moods.

"Turn to page forty-seven."

"We're not on page forty-seven, we're on page forty-eight."

"We're on page forty-seven. I marked it when we stopped last time."

"That's wrong. We're on page forty-eight."

"Don't argue with me. Don't be a troublemaker. Turn to page forty-seven!"

"I'm not a troublemaker. You just don't know what page we're on."

"I know what page we're on. You just have to argue with everything I say."

"I don't argue with everything you say. You argue with everything I say." And on and on.

My students argued too, but I looked for ways to handle it that didn't involve my arguing back. One day I had the following exchange with a student.

"Let's start on page five."

"We're not on page five, we're on page seven."

"Okay, let's read page seven. Start with the top paragraph."

"We're not on the top paragraph, we're on the bottom."

"Okay, read the bottom paragraph."

"That paragraph is boring. I don't want to read it."

"Choose any paragraph."

"Why don't you make up your mind!"

Fortunately, my mood was secure, so I could not only see what was happening, but I could see the humor in it, so that's what I keyed on. I sat back in my chair, smiled and said, "Oh, I get it. It's a game. I say, 'This is black,' and you say, 'No, it's white,' and I say, 'Okay, it's white,' then you say, It's not white, it's fuchsia.' That's an interesting game."

Billy puffed up and said, "I am *not* playing that game. You're wrong." I said, "Oh, really? Perhaps I am wrong. By the way is that a new pencil?" Billy replied, "This is not a pencil, it's a pen." I looked at him and couldn't help but burst out laughing. He looked confused, then slowly his face opened with a sheepish grin of recognition and he said, "I guess I am doing what you said. I didn't know it." I replied, "That's okay, it happens to all of us. It's just a mood," and we continued in a more congenial spirit.

BUT DOES IT WORK?

When my mood was congenial I had obedience without obscenity, compliance without catastrophe, order without offensiveness. We worked hard but we didn't drudge. We racked out brains but kept our sense of humor. We had success without tears, accomplishment without stress.

My students were not only learning to read, they were *liking* it. Many were reading *voluntarily,* outside of class. They were feeling success and because of it, they were changing the way they thought about themselves and what was possible for them. I was enjoying teaching like never before. But one nagging doubt plagued me.

Would my student's posttest scores be as high as the posttest scores of the students in other classes? Students in other classes had a full forty minutes of instruction each lesson. Taking time to modify moods meant my students had less instruction time. On some days, if the mood was hopelessly distracted or if a student showed up sick or exhausted, as was frequently the case, I didn't didn't try to teach concepts at all but read a story aloud while the student rested.

How would the posttests of students who were getting less instruction time, students being taught only when their moods were open, compare with the posttest scores of students taught the traditional way, with no consideration for the state of their minds? That was my question at the end of the year when I nervously compared the difference between my students pre- and posttest scores and the pre- and posttest scores of the other teacher's students. I was shaken by what I found.

My students scored an average of *three times higher* than their peers in all three areas, vocabulary, comprehension and total reading, of the Gates MacGinitie Reading Test[1]. The same thing happened in math. My students' scores weren't just as high as those of their peers. They were higher. Significantly higher. It was a shocker. Since then, I've seen other teachers using this state-dependent approach to learning have similar or even better results.

BUT CAN WE DO IT?

More and more people brought up on the "No pain, no gain" philosophy of life are hearing that small, persistent voice inside that says, "Life wasn't meant to be a struggle." Yet, it takes courage to follow your own wisdom and break the mold. It takes wisdom to slow down to get more done; it takes boldness to orient yourself to human beings instead of the clock. It takes new thinking to turn teaching and learning into a gourmet meal leisurely savored and quietly digested rather than what it is now—a gulp and burp at a fast food place.

Yet, in this hurry-up, go-faster world of ours, we're usually too busy to think of changing moods, or if we think of it, we feel too pressed by time to do it. But when we feel so overwhelmed that we don't think we have time for sanity—so busy that we don't have time to disconnect from what we *don't want* to reconnect with what we *do want*—that's a sure sign we've bought the bad-mood farm ourselves. That's a sure sign it's time to relocate. Our educational system could use some relocation.

When our education system changes, it will be from the inside out, one teacher at a time in one classroom at a time having the courage to realize that what we've been doing isn't working. One teacher at a time giving up the craziness and getting back to the sanity of their original dream—doing good work, giving a helping hand to those coming behind and being enriched by it. One teacher at a time foregoing struggle and teaching joyfully, not only because it's the most humane thing to do, but because it gets the best results possible.

SUMMARY

In positive states the human mind does what it does best—the magnificent, mysterious, magical work of learning, and the results are excellence.

Gearing Up

Intelligence, Thought and States of Mind

Intelligence

Beyond IQ

The idea of a multidimensional intelligence broadens not only our view of human capability, but of learning itself.

Throughout time, enlightened men and women have referenced a level of intelligence that is deeper and more comprehensive than IQ. This is the form of intelligence we call wisdom or common sense, good judgment, level-headedness or perceptive awareness. Principle One of Creating Teachable Moments is: *there are two dimensions of intelligence*: (1) IQ, the acquired fund of information; and (2) wisdom, the deeper more profound innate intelligence.

IQ TESTS

There is no testing instrument better known, nor more misunderstood, than the intelligence test. IQ tests were designed at the turn of the century by Binet and Simon, French psychologists, to identify children unlikely to benefit from classroom instruction. These tests, which measured the subskills considered necessary for classroom success, predicted which students would learn to read and which would fail.

A statistician named Spearman[1] found that Binet and Simon's test had a high correlation with other tests that began to appear and reasoned that the high correlation suggested that all the tests must be measuring the same thing. Spearman named this new concept "g" for general intelligence. Almost immediately, Spearman's construct was challenged by experts, but in spite of heated controversy, the notion of general intelligence became widely-accepted. The idea that you can quantify how bright or dull a person is, is new to this century.

There are many problems basic to using IQ scores. IQ tests only measure the information-processing capability of the brain under certain circumstances. A high IQ doesn't predict whether a person will act intelligently, with sound judgment and common sense. It doesn't predict whether they will be creative or have mental health, self-esteem or well-being. IQ tests only predict how well a person will do on tasks that are similar to the items on the test. The best prediction of a high IQ is that the individual will score high on other intelligence tests.

IQ tests have become, not so much a measure of potential for achievement, but as a measure of achievement itself. A person with an IQ score of 164 is considered to have already achieved more than the person whose score is 110.

IQ tests limit the way people perceive their own and other people's ability to learn. Before IQ tests, people perceived themselves and others as having a more complex range of potential. A person could be good with numbers but poor at writing letters; a creative thinker, but not so good at balancing the checkbook. As IQ tests became widely used, the IQ score became an integral part of a person's self-concept. A person with an IQ of 140 feels differently about herself, about what she can do or be, than she would if she had an IQ of 100. Teachers, parents or counselors, even ones who try not to be biased, think differently, feel differently and behave differently toward a person whose IQ is 150 than they do toward a person whose IQ is 80. This is true even though people frequently perform with greater or lesser capability than their IQ scores indicate they should. This was first apparent to me as a classroom teacher.

A FIRST GRADE TEACHER GRAPPLES WITH THE MYSTERY OF LEARNING

As a first grade teacher, I was struck by the magical way children learn. All youngsters, even the ones with low IQs, managed to grasp concepts far too complicated to be directly transmitted from one person to another. In a school system with no kindergarten, most of the youngsters began the first year not knowing the alphabet or having any idea that letters stood for sounds that formed meaningful words and sentences.

I worried about teaching so many difficult, abstract concepts to wiggling, half-attentive kids with microscopic attention spans; kids whose idea of a good time was to suck water out of the fishbowl with straws left over from lunch. But I forged ahead and by October all the students were reading simple three- and-four word sentences in their new books. By the end of the year, eight months later, all the students, even the ones with low IQ scores, were reading paragraphs of complex sentences with comprehension. They were spelling, doing arithmetic and writing fresh, interesting stories for their parents to display on refrigerator doors, all very complicated, abstract functions. I was amazed. As I watched the children file out the last day of school, I had to admit, all of them, even the slowest, had learned more than I was able to teach.

I taught concepts, such as, 2 + 2 = 4, R-E-D is "red," which is different from R-I-D, which is "rid," and so on. But in order for these abstract concepts to make sense, to have any real meaning, students had to take the magical step from concept to understanding.

FROM CONCEPT TO UNDERSTANDING

The step from concept to understanding is one no teacher can tell students how to take, a step no teacher can take for them, yet every one of those first graders did it. Low IQ, high IQ, it didn't matter. They started with concepts too difficult to articulate and they pushed through to comprehension.

To appreciate how complex this step is, take something every toddler understands, the difference between a dog and a cat. Try writing down an explanation of the concept "dog," then write down how a dog is different from a cat. Then, when you're done, try teaching these concepts to your baby. Fortunately, because of the magical intelligence of your child, you don't have to go through this grief. All you have to do is point to one animal and say, "dog," and point to another and say, "cat," and eventually, after several repetitions, your intelligent offspring will fill the gaps with understanding, thus handily grasping abstract distinctions far too difficult to be passed directly from one person to another.

Most amazing is a baby's ability to grasp the abstractions of speech and language, a learning feat so difficult linguists can't explain how infants do it. Somehow, infants not only pull words out of the thousands of chaotic, run-together sounds they hear swirling around the house, but they understand the subtle meanings those words convey! At three, youngsters are fluent in speech and language though they've never had a lesson, no formal training, no curriculum or tutor. Running around the house chewing on the dog, toddlers effortlessly master the abstract principles of speech of language and every other toddler in the world is doing the same thing. By two years of age, most toddlers know 1,000 words, rules of sentence construction and also the basic hypothesis of language formation!

IQ tests are based on the assumption that there is a hierarchy of skills from simple to complex, the complex skills being those that are more abstract. It is assumed that the simple skills, those that require little understanding, are the easiest to learn and to teach to the young or the intellectually handicapped.

But learning, when it proceeds naturally——like it does for babies and preschoolers——isn't logical, it's magical. The very young and the people we call intellectually handicapped, learn speech and language as babies. What learning is more difficult and abstract than that? Our basic educational assumptions, those upon which IQ tests are based, seriously underestimate the power of the human mind for learning.

Youngsters don't learn in small bites. They gulp whole mouthfuls at once. My no-nonsense third grade teacher, believing in the hierarchy of skills from simple to complex, believing that students had to know the sounds of the alphabet before they could read, led the class in phonetic drills. Although I did this exercise, I didn't see any connection between it and the enjoyable process of reading.

If my first grade teacher had said, "First we'll learn the alphabet names, then we'll learn the sounds and their combinations, then we'll learn the meanings of words and then you will start reading," I would have dropped out of school before Halloween. Fortunately, the first day of school my teacher pointed to a word and said, "This word is 'Sally.'" And I started reading that day. Then in third grade, in another school, already an excellent reader, I learned to recite the phonetic sounds of the alphabet. We haven't even come close to recognizing the ability of human minds, even immature ones or ones with low IQ's, to leap effortlessly from concept to understanding.

A NEW LOOK AT LEARNING

Contemporary learning theories are of two principle types, mechanistic and organic.

Mechanistic Approaches To Learning

Mechanistic approaches to learning see the learner as passive, a blank slate that responds blindly to outside forces. These older, more traditional theories are based on conditioning, stimulus and response, from the work of the Russian psychologist, Ivan Pavlov and his famous salivating dogs.

Pavlov discovered if he rang a bell when he fed his dogs, eventually the animals would salivate at the sound of a bell, even in the absence food. Pavlov called this a "conditioned reflex." An American psychologist, B.F. Skinner, building on Pavlov's theory, defined behavior as being determined by its consequences——rewarded behavior is repeated and punished behavior is stopped. Most contemporary schools are fashioned on this model of reward and punishment. Good behavior and achievement is rewarded with higher marks and advancement to the next grade. Poor behavior and low achievement is punished by low marks or the penalty of repeating a grade. Unfortunately, these practices do little more than confirm a student's self-destructive belief that there is something wrong with him and that he deserves to be punished.

Organic Learning Theories

The newer, organic learning theories, which started developing around the work of Humanistic psychologists such as Abraham Maslow[2] and Carl Rogers[3], focus on the inner, psychological foundations of the learning process. These approaches define learning, not as a passive reaction to outside events, but as an active inner process by which innate potential is actualized. Learners are seen as capable, full participants in the learning process. These theories, focusing on processes, principles and qualitative change, relate learning to motivation, personal needs and feelings; they consider the unpredictable, such as a flash of intuitive insight.

Rather than advocating punishment as a way to change unwanted behavior, these theories hold that punishment (aversive conditioning) can set self-defeating behavior, that people can only change for the better when they feel capable and safe.

Most recent developments in learning theory go a step farther and look at mind-brain-consciousness as an open, whole, dynamic innerconnected system capable of infinite, creative interaction with the environment. The focus of these promising, emerging theories is to expand consciousness to increase the flexibility and fluency of our mental functioning. Table 4-A compares the emphases of traditional and modern learning theories.

Table 4-A
Emphasis of Traditional and Modern Learning Theories

Traditional	Modern
Memorization, Repetition	Understanding, Insight
Conformity	Diversity, Individuality
From Simple To Complex	Open, Creative, Flexible
Static, Ritualized Process	Quality Content
Tedium	Interest, Variety, Pleasure
Reward/Punishment/Failure	Self-Esteem/Safety/Success
Fixed, Static IQ	Dynamic, Multidimensional
Competition, Isolation	Collaboration, Teamwork

When we take a fresh, unbiased look at learning, we realize IQ scores, the mechanistic view of learning and the fundamentals of education we've derived from them, don't account for all of human potential. There is more to human intelligence than IQ. As a scientific field, we must recognize a more profound and true intelligence, a deeper natural intelligence called wisdom.

WISDOM: THE DIMENSION OF KNOWING

Human intelligence is far more vast and dynamic than we have imagined. In addition to having a magnificent biological computer, our IQ, we also have the wonderful capability of wisdom, the deeper, spontaneous awareness that brings effortless knowing, intuition, creativity, insight, inspiration, common sense and good judgment. While both dimensions of intelligence are interconnected and work together as a whole, there are basic differences between them.

IQ is acquired. It is something we learn and store in memory. This includes concepts, beliefs, assumptions, expectations, attitudes and values. IQ is the source of our socialization and conditioning. Because of our learned storehouse of information, we are able to speak our language, balance our checkbook and remember not to drink milk out of the carton when mother is in the room.

IQ functions from memory, our learning in the past. This learning may or may not be factual or even helpful for that matter. For example, at one time the highest IQ's in the world believed that the world was flat, that if you walked too far in one direction, you'd drop over the horizon like a rock. Not too long ago, the highest IQ's believed in using leeches to purify blood and in segregation of the races.

IQ operates through analytic/logical/linear modes of thinking. It involves the vigorous processing of thought content such as remembering, verbalizing, comparing, contrasting, evaluating, differentiating, distinguishing, separating, classifying, ranking and choosing. Calling IQ into play, we say, "Just a minute, let me think," and we stop to figure things out. IQ, the intelligence associated with left brain functioning, has dominated our educational system almost exclusively. Wisdom is the new kid in the educational neighborhood.

Wisdom isn't learned. It is innate, natural. We are born with it. Wisdom is a limitless pool of awareness that exists in each of us. It's there *before* we learn what to think. Wisdom is our first intelligence, unconditioned, universal and objective. It isn't logical by IQ standards. It operates from a higher logic.

"It's easier to run fast if you relax," the coach tells an athlete. A runner in touch with wisdom has a momentary sense of confusion, then he says, "Oh, yeah, that makes sense," Wisdom is not logical in terms of what we've learned in the past, but it comes with an undeniable ring of truth. Running faster by relaxing is a concept that contradicts our beliefs about having to work *hard* to accomplish our goals. IQ says, "Tighten up, strain, push yourself to the edge of exhaustion." Wisdom says, "Relax, glide, run within yourself and you'll do better."

Wisdom is a puzzle. When I first heard, whispered secretly by the older kids in the back room of a country schoolhouse, what the f-word meant, it didn't come as a shock. I thought to myself, "I knew that." It puzzled me that I knew something I'd never heard before. But before I heard it said, I didn't know that I knew it! This is what teachers do. They say things students already know somewhere deep inside themselves, so they can recognize them. Think of it. How would it be possible to learn something that isn't already part of our consciousness! When we say, "Oh! I see!" what could be seen except something that had been there all along, unrecognized?

Recognizing wisdom when we hear it outside ourselves is one thing. Calling it up within ourselves is something else again. Activating our own wisdom is tricky because wisdom is *not* activated through analytic/logical/linear thinking, the mode of thinking we've been taught to use exclusively.

Because wisdom exists before and outside of our thought system, it knows what thought is doing. Wisdom can see when we are using thought against ourselves, producing distressing or self-limiting ideas that are getting in our way. Wisdom allows us to see, evaluate and change thinking patterns that are not serving us well. Wisdom allows us to direct thought rather than being directed by it.

Walking through the forest, surrounded by tall trees, one can get lost. But if you go to the top of a hill you see rivers, fences and roads, landmarks you couldn't see from below, making it easier to find your way. Likewise, from the higher vantage point of wisdom, we see our thought system, our thinking, feelings, perceptions and behaviors with an objectivity that is impossible when we are looking from the inside, out. Wisdom takes us to a higher level of consciousness.

Wisdom isn't what we learn, but the ability to learn. Wisdom isn't what we think, but the ability to think as we choose. Wisdom isn't our conditioning, the beliefs, the interpretations of life we learned from our family, friends and society. Wisdom is the ability to see our conditioning as the product of our thinking and to change it if we want to. Wisdom is not a philosophy, but the understanding that all philosophies are outgrowths of observation and that observations are related to and inseparable from thinking.

We've been taught that if we have certain information and skills, if we do well in school and get good grades, we are intelligent. Yet, information and skills without the wisdom to use them prudently, is of no value. It's of no value to pass a test on parenting if you go home and beat the kids. You may have memorized the list of presidents in order, but wisdom advises against reciting it during a candlelight dinner with your sweetheart.

We get just so far in our conceptualization, then we run into things our analytic thinking can't grasp, like how to live a kind, loving life or how to know who we are and why we are here. We are more than brains, more than biological computers. We are living, breathing human beings. We run mental programs so effortlessly that, caught up in the drama, we forget we are also the programmer, the operator, camera, projector, director, principal actor and critic creating the drama.

To raise our level of consciousness, to awaken wisdom in ourselves and others we have to know it's there, to look for it, to be open ourselves to ever-deepening experience, just like we did when we were youngsters and thought was open, a magic carpet to wisdom, the land of joyful, effortless knowing.

WHO HAS WISDOM?

Every thinking person has wisdom. All people, whatever age, sex, race, culture, education, IQ or station in life, are born capable of a seeing that goes beyond vision and a hearing that goes beyond sound. We're all capable of spontaneous all-at-once knowledge that doesn't come directly from logical, analytical thinking. Children have as much access to wisdom as adults. Women have as much as men. Maids have as much as supreme court justices. People in isolated, primitive tribes have as much capability for wisdom as people in technologically advanced countries. Students, clients, and youngsters all have wisdom; so do teachers, counselors and parents.

Our deepest challenge, our most profound opportunity as teachers, counselors and parents is more than just passing on information and teaching analytical thinking skills. Our greater challenge is to realize the deep learning capability of the human mind, whatever the measured IQ score. There are no untalented students, only teachers who haven't yet discovered how to bring their talent out. This takes wisdom.

Wisdom, unlike information, can't be passed directly from one person to another. It can't be found in books; it can't be memorized or found through mental struggle. Wisdom emerges from within ourselves when analytical thinking is still. Wisdom is direct, first-hand knowing that comes through the experience of *in*sight.

WISDOM ON A PRACTICAL LEVEL

Your sixteen-year-old daughter comes home three hours late and your first impulse is to ground her the rest of her life. Wisdom cautions: wait for a better idea. So you give yourself time for the mental dust to settle. When fear subsides and your mind is calm, you remember what it's like to be sixteen. In touch with a deeper, more compassionate understanding, in touch with your love, you see how to proceed in ways that brings you closer to your daughter rather than pushing you farther apart. Wisdom is knowing when to wait for a better answer and recognizing inspiration when it comes.

It used to be that teachers taught information. But trying to teach kids the essential information they need in the twenty-first century is an impossible task. How can a high school science teacher keep up with information when the base of biogenetics doubles every four months? It's time teachers broadened their scope and started teaching students how to learn, how to use their biological computers and when to set them aside and wait for wisdom.

A master teacher helps students get in touch, not just with their measured ability for analytical thinking and problem solving, but with their unmeasurable deeper intelligence, their common sense and wisdom, the magical dimension of intelligence through which they learned speech and language as babies.

We've gotten so used to mental struggle, to memorization, to conceptual, logical, step-by-step thinking, we think that's all there is to learning. We've gotten so used to defining ourselves by our IQ score; we think that's all there is to our capability. But IQ tests don't measure the ability to think, which is limitless; they measure the concepts, the products of our thinking to date. IQ tests don't measure the ability for understanding, intuition, inspiration and wisdom, which, when our thought and intelligence are working together properly as they did then we were children, is virtually unlimited.

For all our new knowledge about the brain, the mind remains a mystery. The brain is a body part, like the liver or heart. Something more profound than the heart makes it beat and something more profound than the brain makes it work.

Consciousness and awareness are the deepest mysteries of life. Intelligent, dynamic, active, indefinable, closer to us than the air we breathe, as present as sunshine. Our capacity for wisdom—for learning, growing and changing—is virtually unlimited. Our responsibility and challenge now as teachers is to learn how to tap these rich internal resources.

SUMMARY

Human beings are born with an innate intelligence for learning that is evidenced in early learning but not reflected in IQ scores. This deeper, more profound intelligence is called wisdom. Wisdom enables babies to penetrate the secrets of speech and language while ingesting hugh amounts of carpet lint. It is what enables us to take the magical step from concept to understanding.

Learning is most effective when we use the full range of our multi-dimensional powers. IQ is the acquired storehouse of information activated through logical, step-by-step thinking. Wisdom is the intelligent awareness that slips into thought when analytical thinking takes a more passive role. Sometimes we have to get the brain out of the way so we can learn. Knowing when to get the brain out of the way so we can learn is an activity of wisdom.

5

Wisdom

in Action

Mental health is more than the absence of insanity.

There is an inborn level of consciousness in human beings that is deeper than the content of our thinking. A truly objective psychological realm exists one step before thinking, a core intelligence that we call wisdom or common sense, an irrepressible drive to learn that never stops pushing for expression. Having the light of recognition dawn in yourself or seeing it in the eyes of a student are two of the most rewarding experiences a teacher can have.

Usually we think of learning as originating out there, in a teacher, book or class; but learning happens inside. Without an inner understanding, outer details have no meaning. A teacher writes on the board: "2 + 2 = 4," and at first this strange equation has no meaning for students. But eventually the penny drops, the inner light goes on and the student says, "Aha! Now I get it!" That's knowing. It's *in*sight, a sight within. It's really quite miraculous. We are the source of our own learning.

KNOWING IN CHILDREN

The facility of knowing is present in children. Alice tells this story about her son, Brian.

When Brain was two, I discovered he had a way of knowing things. One night, dressing for bed, he asked, "Why do I wear a night-diaper? I don't wear diapers during the day?" I explained, "It's easier to know when you have to go the bathroom during the day than it is at night when you're asleep. Your diaper's wet every morning, so I know you still need one at night. Brian, quiet, closed his eyes and went inside himself. It was a way he had.

He'd shut his eyes and get still. I liked watching him do it. It seemed like such a grown-up thing to do. Then, he opened his eyes and said, "I don't need a night-diaper anymore." Of course I didn't believe him. It wasn't logical. Skeptical, but prompted by some deeper, inner instinct of my own, I put him to bed for the first time without a diaper. The next morning and every morning after that, he woke up dry as a Sahara sand dune. This two year old not only knew, he knew he knew.

A Counselor Learns From Wise Children

Children can be quite wise. One morning Richard, a student counselor working with emotionally disturbed children, came to group depressed. The children, picked up on his feelings and asked "What's wrong." Richard said, "Last night in class people watched videos of my work then spent an hour telling me everything I was doing wrong. When they were through, I felt like I wasn't doing a good job."

The children were very tuned in. One of them said, "You shouldn't listen to what other people say about you." Another said, "You are a nice person, just remember that." And, another, "Yeah, they were probably just in a bad mood." And, like a scratch that's been kissed, Richard felt better.

One minute kids are banging on the piano with the turtle, then, when you least expect it, they change into clear-eyed sages, heros and warriors whose wisdom stops you dead in your tracks. But everybody, even adults, can be wise when they go to that quiet place inside where wisdom resides. I remembered this years later working with Mickey.

Mickey: A Girl Who Forgot the Secret to Knowing

Mickey was sixteen. Golden hair, liquid-blue eyes and lashes out to here, charming and popular, Mickey had the reading skills of a second grader. The first time we met, Mickey said, "I'm not smart. Everyone calls me an air head, but I don't mind. I always have a date on Saturday night."

There was nothing wrong with Mickey's intelligence, but she thought there was and that was the problem. The key to unlocking Mickey's potential was to get her to think differently about herself as a reader. We started reading fashion magazines because that was the only reading that interested her, eventually moving to other books geared to her interests. One day Mickey admitted, "Reading isn't too-too bad," and I knew we were on the right track, for truly this was a new thought. Then it was time for a test.

Mickey stared at the dreaded booklet, her newfound good feelings lost in unhappy memories of the past. Seeing her fighting back tears, I knew she'd given up before she got started. I said, "Mickey, you've learned more in the last few weeks than you know. Relax, do your best and you may be surprised." Resigned, she opened the booklet and began.

Mickey finished the vocabulary portion of the test and began the comprehension section. For this section of the exam, Mickey read a prepared segment of text. Then I asked her questions about it to test her understanding. She answered the first questions, the easy ones, correctly; then I asked one that required her to make an inference. Her face went blank. "I don't know. I just don't know. I never could do this right." Tears welled up.

I said, "Mickey, the answer to this question isn't in the words you read. The answer is common sense, something you would just *know* from reading. I said, "Relax, close your eyes and go inside to a place where your thought is quiet. That's where the answer will be."

She closed her eyes and became still. After a bit, her face lit up and she said, "John made that remark because he was angry but didn't want Susan to know it." The perfect answer. When I congratulated her, she said, "I didn't know about that place inside.

That's cool." After that, every time I asked Mickey a question she didn't know, she got quiet, closed her eyes, went inside and then came out with an astute answer. She was surprised. "Why didn't somebody tell me about this before," she asked.

Mickey hadn't been told because then, 1984, psychology was just waking up to the fact that there is a wisdom inside human beings, a level of consciousness that tells you things you need to know when logic fails. Discovering the "smart place," as Mickey called it, was a turning point. She wanted to know more.

"Why am I smarter here than I am in my other classes?" she asked. I replied, "You're smart here because you're relaxed, interested in what you're doing and paying attention. When that happens, your mind opens and your thought connects to your smart place. Mickey said, "That's cool."

In twenty hours of lessons, Mickey, the air head, mastered three years of reading. Eventually, she caught up to her class. The last time I talked to Mickey, she was applying to colleges to study fashion design.

There's an old saying that if you give a person a fish, he will eat once but if you teach him how to catch fish, he will eat the rest of his life. You can tell your students, clients and youngsters what to do or you can teach them where their own wisdom comes from so they will always know what to do, even when you aren't there to tell them.

Janie Said, "I Didn't Do It"

Myra's sixteen year old daughter, Janie, was stealing money to buy drugs. Faced with indisputable evidence, Janie looked Myra right in the eye and said, "I didn't do it." Myra was terrified.

Myra approached the problem rationally, doing all the things she'd learned in the past. First, she reasoned with Janie, told her all the reasons it was harmful to take drugs, to steal and to lie. Throughout the lecture, Janie sat like a zombie and afterward she'd said, "I didn't do it."

When that didn't work, Myra restricted Janie's activities, put her on a strict schedule and gave her increased responsibilities at home. The stealing continued. Myra was consumed with worry. The minute Janie came in the door, it was all Myra could do not to blurt out, "Did you steal anything today? Did you take drugs?" Myra told Janie repeatedly that she loved her and when that didn't work, she screamed it in her face, but nothing penetrated Janie's grunt and shrug attitude.

Myra talked to other parents, neighbors, teachers, to her own parents, but no one had any new ideas. She called a psychologist, a friend, and he said, "Myra, I'll see Janie if you want me to, but the truth is, I see lots of teenagers. Sometimes counseling helps and sometimes it doesn't. Frankly, my batting average with kids in this situation isn't all that great."

Myra barely slept and had no appetite. The whole family was under such tremendous stress, Myra dreaded going home at night. Then something inexplicable happened. Myra tells it this way:

Driving to work one morning, I slipped a Mozart tape into the tape deck. The music was so beautiful that for the first time in weeks I forgot Janie and luxuriated in the splendor of the moment. Transported in that wonderful feeling, I suddenly knew exactly what to do about Janie. It was so clear, I couldn't believe I hadn't seen it before.

Although it's impossible to put into words all I saw in that moment, I knew everything would be fine. I'd taught Janie everything I could and now it was up to her to work this out in her own way. It was her life, her path, her opportunity, her learning. She would do what she would do, I had no control over that. But, whatever she chose, her life and mine were bound together in some lovely way, and always would be, no matter what. I can't describe the peace that moment gave me. I wasn't afraid anymore.

I called my husband and said, "Honey, we've been going about it all wrong. Keeping things stirred up at home has only made a bad situation worse. We need to let Janie know that we love her and are there for her, but now that she's living her own life, making her own decisions, her behavior is something she controls, not us. We've got to stop trying to change her so she'll have the space to change herself when she's ready. We need to settle down and make our home a happy, healthy place again. That's how we can help her the most." He said, "That sounds right to me," and that's what we did. Our home became a happy place again and, things eventually worked out just fine for Janie.

Myra, in a moment of mental quiet, had an *in*sight, a moment of knowing, that took away her fear and showed her she needed to give Janie the opportunity to rely on her own wisdom. When I heard Myra's story, I asked her how it turned out and she said, "Once we pulled our wind out of Janie's sails and she knew she was responsible for her own actions, she started behaving differently, better at home, more like her old self. When she started asking our advice, we encouraged her to look inside herself to see what made the best sense to her, then we'd talk it over. I got one more call from the school, but that was the last. Janie's a grown woman now, quite responsible, with a career and children of her own."

Wisdom is always there when compulsive thinking is stilled, as I learned from Davey, the angriest boy I ever met.

Davey, The Angriest Boy I Ever Met

When I met Davey, he looked small, broken and torn, out of place in the cheery waiting room. The muscles of Davey's face and shoulders tightened and jerked involuntarily every few seconds. Silent, staring vacantly at the floor, banging his scruffy untied sneakers on the chair leg, Davey seemed lost in a world of his own.

Eight-year-old Davey was referred to the clinic for threatening to stab his teacher with a pair of scissors, bullying other students, and refusing to listen or do his assignments. Davey had no friends, no place where he fit in. His thick psychiatric file documented a long history of severe emotional disturbance.

As a new counselor I wondered how I could help this deeply troubled child. Nothing in my training told me how to make a broken boy well. The only things that gave me the courage to try were his great need and my strong intuitive belief that something inside Davey, some vital, still healthy part of him held the blueprint for his health. Inspired by the innovative work of

Virginia Axline[1], Clark Moustakas[2] and Carl Rogers[3] people whose humanistic work was based on belief in an inner self-correcting mechanism, an ever-present drive toward self-actualization and mental health, I found the courage to trust the wisdom I couldn't see to restore emotional balance.

A nondirective play therapist provides children with a safe playroom, a variety of toys and a supportive, nonjudgmental, non-interfering environment where, through "playing out" their fears, hatred, loneliness, neglect, abuse, failure and desperation, youngsters come to terms with health in their own way. As a play therapist I did not initiate conversation or suggest activities. Not there as a personality in my own right, but as a mirror for Davey, I, by making observations, reflected or supported only what he initiated. My role was to give Davey's health a place to work itself out and be there to support it along the way. I trusted this part of Davey to create his own design for wellness. Surely a child's mental health couldn't be lost. It must be hiding somewhere nearby.

I tell Davey's story, not to illustrate the technique of non-directive play therapy, but to show how Davey's unfailing creative inner resource, his wisdom, guided him back to mental health.

Davey lived with his mother and seven brothers and sisters in a run-down house in a run-down neighborhood. His mother, a melancholy woman with a weighty psychiatric file of her own, gave permission for Davey's counseling but refused to be involved herself.

In the playroom the first day I explained, "Play with the toys as you please. I will not allow you to hurt yourself or me and you cannot break the windows." He walked around the sunny room cautiously, touching the puppets, the dolls, the dress-up clothes, the water pistol and the sand box. He picked up the plastic baby bottle, asked, "What's this?" and wrinkled his nose and threw the bottle to the floor with a disgusted look. He picked up the rubber knife and threatened to hit me with it. "You would like to hit me with the knife but it's against the rules." He set the toy knife down and went around the room, examined every toy, saying nothing. When he did speak, his speech was interrupted by the same involuntary spasms as his body. When time was up, he simply walked out the door without a word. That was the last calm for weeks.

The next week Davey started up the stairway to our second-floor playroom screaming curses. He exploded into the playroom like a hundred hurricanes. I gulped and thought, "Oh, health, please be in there somewhere," as Davey raged through the room overturning tables, chairs, boxes of clothes—anything, everything in his path. He hurled dolls against the walls, threw sand, tried to bite the rubber soldiers in two, dumped a pile of small cars and trucks in the middle of the room and stomped up and down on them screaming a combination of curses and raw sounds with an energy that left me breathless. He stopped, picked up a puppet and threatened to throw it at me. "Throw the puppet if you want, but not at me."

Redirected, Davey picked up an armful of puppets and heaved them violently against the wall. After forty minutes of driving activity, Davey collapsed in a small heap in the sandbox, hair stuck to his wet forehead. After a moment, I sat beside him and ventured an observation, "You're really, really angry inside." He whispered, "I'm a scalding hot, fiery furnace, burning up inside." When Davey left that day, the room looked like a fiery furnace had passed through. The next four weeks were the same. Davey exploded screaming into the room, destroyed it for an hour, then, when time was up, he turned and walked away.

There were a few hopeful signs. Davey's teacher said although he still refused to do any work, he was calmer, more manageable in the classroom. Both his teacher and I noticed his facial tics and stuttering had lessened.

The fifth week Davey came into the playroom strangely quiet —nervous, agitated. After looking nervously around the room he asked, "Can anyone see us?" After assurances that we were quite alone, he drew down the window shade, pulled a blue gingham dress out of the clothes box and put it on over his tattered blue jeans. He said quietly, looking at the floor, "My name is Nancy and I'm a girl. You are mom."

My mind whirred. "Oh, my God, a sexual identity crisis. He's getting worse, not better. What's happening? What should I do?" But, wisdom prevailed; this was Davey's journey, not mine. I could only trust that this boy, in his own way, was doing what he needed to do to restore his emotional balance. So, following Davey's lead, for the next five weeks I was "mom" and Davey was "Nancy." He'd tell me what to do and I did it. "Stand here. Say this. Do that." If I pushed in a direction he was unwilling to go or reflected a feeling inaccurately, he'd either ignore me or say, "No, not now." It was reassuring to know I couldn't make a mistake that would interfere with Davey's work. Then in the tenth week, everything changed again.

Davey entered the room, drew the shade, turned off the light, locked the door and silently paced the room. Finally, as usual, Davey put on the dress, only this time he rummaged through the box until he found a large cloth, which he brought to me and said, "This is a diaper. Pin it on me." Pinning the cloth over Davey's faded jeans, insecurity flooded my thoughts, "Regression. He's going backwards! What should I do now?" But relaxing beyond the intellect to a deeper wisdom, I took a deep breath and pinned on the diaper.

Davey said, "Now, I'm Baby Nancy. You're still mom." "Baby Nancy" sucked on the baby bottle and directed "mom" to fix clay cakes, talk on the phone, clean the house or sit and watch as he played in the sandbox or curled up with a blanket. After several weeks of this activity, "Baby Nancy" directed "mom" into the big refrigerator box. He said, without looking at me, "Sit here." And then he sat beside me playing with toy cars. We touched, arm to arm, for the first time, but no conversation. This pattern continued for several weeks.

Checking with Davey's teacher, I found he was no longer threatening or hurting, his tics and stuttering were gone, but he was still a desperately unhappy little boy, a loner who made no effort to fit in, to talk to people or do his assignments.

Then one day Davey walked into the playroom and his face and body distorted by spasms. He could barely articulate words. My heart knotted as I watched him lock the door, turn out the lights, pull the blinds and put on the dress and diaper. Then, looking down, he said, in a voice disturbingly quiet, "Mom, come into the box with Baby Nancy." We sat side-by-side in the refrigerator box, touching arm to arm, unspeaking until Davey broke the silence. Stuttering heavily, he said, "In a few minutes I will leave and go where you can't come. You stay here. I have something to do but you can't help. I'll call you but you must not come. Promise me, even when I call, even if I beg, you will not come." Frightened, praying Davey knew what he was doing, I promised.

Davey left the box and shut it behind him. Silence. Then moaning, thrashing, wrestling sounds. He cried, "Mommy, help me!" My heart stopped. I longed to run to him, but I could not. "Please mommy, help me." I couldn't breathe. The calling stopped. I could hear my heartbeat reverberating against the cardboard walls. Finally, small sounds I couldn't identify. I waited.

Davey filled the doorway of the box. The dress and diaper were gone. He was looking at me, clear-eyed with a presence and confidence I'd never seen before. He said, in the clearest, steadiest voice I've ever heard, "Baby Nancy is gone. So is Nancy. I am a boy now. I'm Davey." He looked directly into my eyes and in a moment I will never forget, he said, "Hello, Darlene." Long, long moments passed before I could find the voice to answer, "Hello, Davey."

After that day Davey frequently wanted to leave the playroom and take walks in the spring air. We watched pink hyacinth poking out of brown earth and enjoyed the fluffy clouds filling the sky. We saw birds building nests and later, feeding their young. Sometimes we were silent, sharing a world too full for words, other times he asked questions, "What makes flowers grow? What is love? Where do the clouds come from?" He wanted to know, "Are we friends? How do you know? I've never had a friend before."

When we stayed in the playroom, we painted pictures, made sand castles and talked. When Davey remembered sad things, which he sometimes did, he cried in my arms, letting the sadness go. One day he said, "I wish you were my mother." I smiled, "I'd like that too," I said. After a few moments silence, Davey said, "My mother has problems, but she does the best she can. I help her now, so things are better." I marveled. Davey didn't judge. He loved.

June was coming, and with it the end of our time together. One day, walking in the grey Oregon mist, Davey said, "We'll say good-bye won't we? And then we'll never see each other again." I thought, "How brave you are to look unflinchingly into something so tender," and said, "Yes, in a few weeks, we'll say good-bye." Thoughtful for a moment, then he looked at me and said, "I'm glad you were my first friend," and he let go of my hand to chase a grasshopper through the tall grass.

6

Two Dimensions

of Thought

The ability to think and to understand what we are doing is our most important resource.

A group of fifty junior high school teachers were asked, "What psychological activity are you engaged in, no matter what you are doing, working or playing, waking or sleeping?"

The educators were silent. After a few moments, they were given a clue, "This psychological activity is something you are doing right now." More silence. Then a tentative voice from the back of the room, "Is it thinking?" These educators' attention had been drawn to the most profound, yet most overlooked, psychological truth of all time: we think.

Not only do we think, but what we think affects every aspect of our experience. The quality of our life is directly proportional to the quality of our thinking. Everything we perceive or feel, everything we say or do originates in thought. Teaching begins as a thought. So does learning. Ability takes form in thought. So does disability. Self-esteem is a function of thinking. So is self-doubt. Success begins as thought. So does failure. When teaching is difficult and unrewarding, the problem isn't teaching but what we think about teaching. When learning is tedious and troublesome, the problem isn't learning but what we think about learning. Mental blocks, discouragement, poor performance and lackluster achievement all result from faulty thinking.

I've asked the thinking riddle in classes of educators, counselors, parents, physicians, managers, attorneys, people from all walks of life, and found that people——even bright, professional ones——are basically unaware of the fact that they are thinking or that what they are thinking is having an impact on their life!

This is unthinkable. A thinker going through the day unaware of thought is as handicapped as a doctor practicing medicine unaware of microbes or a sailor navigating the sea oblivious of ocean currents. Understanding the role thought plays in our experience is the beginning of wisdom, the key to maximizing potential in ourselves and others.

To be a knowledgeable thinker, mentally prepared for the challenges of teaching and learning, we must know Principle Two of Creating Teachable Moments: *thought has two dimensions*:

1. the ability to think, and
2. the content——ideas, assumptions, judgments——that comes from using this ability.

TWO DIMENSIONS OF THOUGHT

Thought is a single mechanism with dual functions. Babies are born with the ability to think. They come into the world *able* to think, but they don't know *what* to think. From the outset, we see the ability to think is a function separate and apart from the thought content we produce using this ability.

The ability to think——to make up thoughts——is a human being's ultimate creative act. The ability to use this creative force consciously is a human being's ultimate power. Yet, most people think without giving any thought to what they are doing. Most people, like the educators mentioned earlier, are only subliminally aware of their thoughts. This is understandable. Thinking is such an integral part of our moment-to-moment experience, we rarely step back to see what it is and how it affects our life.

THOUGHT CONTENT TAKES MANY FORMS

Thought content takes many forms. Many thought-forms are so subtle, they don't seem like thought at all. Table 6-1 is a partial list of the forms thought takes.

Table 6-1
Forms Thought Takes

Agreement	Diagnosis	Mandates
Assumptions	Disagreement	Notions
Beliefs	Dogmas	Obligation
Bias	Doubt	Observations
Bigotry	Estimates	Obstacles
Choice	Expectations	Opinions
Comprehension	Hunches	Options
Concepts	Ideas	Personal Reality
Conclusions	Images	Philosophies
Conjectures	Imagination	Possibilities
Convictions	Impressions	Prejudice
Creativity	Inferences	Presumption
Creeds	Insight	Stereotypes
Decisions	Interpretations	Suspicion
Deductions	Intuition	Theories
Desire	Judgments	Viewpoints
Determination	Labels	Will-power

Eskimos have hundreds of words to describe forms of snow. We have hundreds of words to describe forms of thought. Knowledgeable thinkers, besides recognizing the *forms* of thought, also recognize that thinking produces immediate emotional and behavioral *results*. We don't think in a vacuum. What we think produces perceptions, emotions and behaviors. What we see, what we feel and what we do is a by-product, a side effect of what we think.

EMOTIONAL AND BEHAVIORAL RESULTS OF THINKING

Table 6-2 and 6-3 is a partial list of the emotional and behavioral results of the act of thinking.

Table 6-2
Emotional Results of the Act of Thinking

Affection	Hate	Moods
Animosity	Hope	Optimism
Cheerfulness	Hostility	Pessimism
Compassion	Indifference	Self-doubt
Depression	Insecurity	Self-esteem
Disappointment	Inspiration	Skepticism
Discouragement	Lethargy	Trust
Enthusiasm	Love	Well-being

Table 6-3
Behavioral Results of the Act of Thinking

Cheating	Giving Up	Opposition
Cooperation	Helpfulness	Participation
Crying	Hostility	Patience
Failure	Interrupting	Sarcasm
Friendliness	Kindness	Smiling
Frowning	Listening	Success
Generosity	Lying	Teamwork

Thought is the center, the core of a human being's experience. Everything we see, everything we feel, everything we say and do originates in thought. The chair you are sitting on started as a thought in someone's mind, so did the building you live in and the car that you drive. What you eat for dinner tonight will be on the table because of what someone thought. How you feel now is a result of what you're thinking. What you do next will be your thought taking form. Behavior is thought made visible. Thought is an immense power. There are serious penalties for thinking without knowing what you are doing. But most people have no idea where thought comes from.

WHERE DOES THOUGHT COME FROM?

Nine year old Tracy came to counseling suffering from insomnia. When his counselor, Cam, asked Tracy why he couldn't sleep, Tracy lowered his eyes and said quietly, "I'm afraid to go to sleep because there are ghosts under my bed." As soon as Tracy said that, Cam knew he had a thought problem, not a ghost problem. He said, "Tracy, I have good news for you! There are no ghosts under your bed. You only *think* there are. Those ghosts are merely figments of your imagination." Tracy's red-rimmed eyes opened wide, "What do you mean?" he asked.

Cam said, "When I was your age I thought a Night-Monster lived in my closet and when the light went out he would sneak out and eat my feet. Then I discovered it was just my imagination working overtime." Tracy said, "But the ghosts seem so real. I can't believe they are just my imagination." Cam said, "Tracy, thought is a wonderful power. With it, you can think anything you want. You can make up dreadful things or wonderful things and because of the magic of thought, whatever you think, if you believe it, it seems real. That's the way thought works."

Tracy said, "My ghosts are thoughts! I can't believe it. Are you sure?" When Cam assured him he was quite certain, Tracy was quiet for a moment, then his face lit up. He said, "If those ghosts are thoughts, that means if I stop thinking them, they will go away!" With that insight, Tracy cured his own insomnia.

The next week, sleeping normally again, Tracy said, "I've discovered I can make up ghosts that are scary or friendly, big or little; I can make them do anything I want and when I want, I can make them disappear." Tracy was learning things about his thinking function that would serve him every day of his life. To make sure he understood the most important point, Cam asked, "Tracy, where do your thoughts come from?" The boy pondered seriously for a few seconds, then he said, "From God."

Tracy didn't fully grasp that *he* was the thinker, *he* was the creative intelligence behind his thoughts. It's a natural mistake. When we think without knowing what we are doing, it seems that thought is something that happens to us, something that acts on us from some outside source. When we don't know better, thought seems to have a mind of it's own, separate from the thinker. But this is impossible. Without a thinker to think, there would be no thought, no one to be aware of thinking.

Twenty-five-year-old Glenda told the counselor, "Each morning I wake up doubting that I'm in the right profession. I don't want to leave teaching. I like it and I'm good at it, but I keep wondering if I made the right career choice." Glenda was relieved to know that her doubts were not premonitions, something acting on her from some esoteric, outside source, they were simply ideas," the end products of her own thinking in a insecure state of mind. Realizing this, Glenda relaxed, took a step back from her agitated ideation and when the mental mud settled, she felt at home in her chosen profession.

Thinking is so effortless, so constant, that like a clock ticking in the background, we tend to forget it's there. More importantly, we tend to forget that thinking is something we are doing. But forgetting that we are thinking, we lose touch with the most powerful part of ourselves. We become onesided, like the painter who identifies with his paintings instead of with his genius to create art, or like the beachcomber who credits the sunset for being beautiful rather than crediting herself for recognizing its beauty. When we forget we are thinking, we identify with our beliefs and opinions rather than with our ability to formulate beliefs and opinions to suit ourselves. When we identify with our beliefs and opinions and overlook the creative intelligence, the mastermind, the thinker behind those thoughts, we trap ourselves on one level of consciousness and end up feeling like the victim of unhappy circumstances.

Feeling Like a Victim of Circumstances Beyond Your Control

Our experience, whatever it is, originates inside, an outgrowth of our thinking. Something happens, and we think about it. And what we think about it determines how we feel and behave in response to it. Since no two people think exactly alike, no two people have the same experience.

Two people sit side-by-side at the movie. One person thinks the film is wonderful, leaves feeling inspired and advises everyone to see it. The other person thinks the film is terrible, leaves feeling cheated and advises everyone not to see it. These two people are mugged by a street gang who takes all their money. One person, thinking one way, feels unlucky, fearful about the future. The other person, thinking another way, feels lucky to get out alive, optimistic about the future. Two people. Two thought systems. Two separate realities.

When we don't know our experience starts *in here*, with what we're thinking, it seems to originate *out there*, in the situation, beyond our control. Feeling the victim of circumstances beyond our control creates feelings of helplessness. It takes away our power of choice.

Amanda, the Unconscious Thinker

It's 7:30 A.M. and Amanda is rushing around the house doing last minute chores. Seven-year-old Todd, announces, "Mommy, I told Miss Spriggs I'd bring cookies and Kool-Aid for the party today." Todd's statement sends icycles through Amanda's spine. She thinks, "This isn't fair. It's too much. I can't cope. Why me?

Thinking this way Amanda feels overwhelmed, victimized. Past injustices flood her thoughts. Future outrages are envisioned. Her blood pressure skyrockets. Her temper spikes. Her finger points. Feeling powerless and trying desperately to gain control, Amanda accuses, attacks, pontificates. Todd runs into the closet and slams the door. The dog hides under the bed. The bird cowers at the bottom of his cage.

Amanda's not to blame. She has no choice. If she had a choice, if she knew she could sidestep her hysterical thinking, she'd choose a better way. Rather than giving way to self-defeating thoughts, Amanda would take a deep breath and open her mind to new thought. With new thought comes new possibilities.

In a moment of mental clarity, Amanda would realize, "It's okay. It's unexpected and inconvenient, but it's not the end of the world. These things happen, especially in second grade, and honestly, to tell the truth, I wouldn't want to miss it for anything. I'll take care of it on my lunch break. I think it will actually be fun." Amanda makes a mental note to teach Todd, in a quieter moment, how to let her know ahead of time when he's made commitments that involve her, but by breaking with her crazy-making thinking, Amanda already teaches Todd a most important lesson: *the unexpected can be handled without a break in sanity.*

If our conditioning——our associations from past experien-ces——have been negative, our habitual thoughts will be negative. In the past, Amanda has been conditioned to think she can't handle unexpected situations without a mental meltdown. So when things come from her blindside, she panics, her thoughts create a storm and she gets lost. If her conditioning had been on the positive side, her thoughts would be more positive. But in either case, thought running on automatic pilot is not the servant but the master.

The secret to choice——to personal power——is to realize that you, the thinker, have the power to separate from any thought that makes you feel weak, or confused. You have the power to change your mind, to let the mud settle so the water will clear. Then you will know what to do. It took Edison 1010 tries to make the light bulb. When someone asked him, "Wasn't it discouraging to fail 1009 times," Edison is reported to have replied, "I didn't fail. Perfecting the light bulb was a process that took 1010 steps." No wonder Edison was a success. Look at the way he thought about what he was doing.

We can't always choose the circumstances of our lives; things happen and we have no say about it. Even when we know we are thinking, much thought content appears automatically, with no conscious effort on our part. However, when we know we are the active thinker behind all our thought——no idea is in our mind without our participation——we become a more active participant in life. We ask, "Does this thought serve me? Does it bring out the best in myself or others? Does it create hostility or cooperation? Does it contribute to my well-being and the well-being of others?" If the train of thought is headed in a positive direction, we follow it. If it is headed toward disaster, we separate from it, clear our mind and wait for the wisdom to see a better way.

We think constantly. We can't help it. A conscious thinker, like a conscious shopper, picks, chooses, ignores and discards. Choosing which thoughts to follow and which to let go is the most important decision a thinker makes. Thinkers who don't know they're thinking, those limited to one level of consciousness, can't make these decisions. All they can do is think the way they've been conditioned to think in the past and suffer the perceptual, emotional and behavioral consequences of that thinking without hope for change.

If we've been conditioned to think that driving in traffic is stressful, we have no choice but to be tense driving on the interstate. If we've been conditioned to think that Mondays are depressing, we have no choice but to feel blue at the beginning of the week. However, when we know that experience begins in thought, we become an active, interested participant in our thinking process. We can change our mind, play with new possibilities and discover—to our delight—that we can be happy, even on a rainy Monday, driving in heavy traffic, or taking all three kids home from school with chicken pox. When we know we're thinking, mental breakdowns are optional. If we don't know we're thinking, we not only blindly suffer the consequences of our own self-limited thinking, but we fall victims to other people's negative ideas as well. Rather than being active thinkers in our own right, we become passive receptacles for other people's ideas.

Being Passive Receptacles for Other People's Ideas

Once, the most advanced thinkers believed the world was flat. Now, most people think differently. Tomorrow, if we are open to it, we will realize even deeper levels of understanding than we see today. When students know that ideas, beliefs, discoveries, inventions, theories and philosophies are the result of people's thinking to date, these youngsters are inspired to go beyond being memorizers, receptacles of other people's ideas, and to be creative thinkers in their own right. Ignorance is not a lack of information. It's being unaware of the fact of thinking.

It's important to learn historically what people's thinking has been and what that thinking has accomplished, good and bad, to date. It's empowering and inspiring to see people's earlier thinking as a starting place, something we can evaluate and discard, contribute to or advance beyond. Someone observed that kids in this country come to school as question marks and leave as periods. Current educational practice keeps kids so busy learning other people's ideas, regurgitating them on tests then memorizing more, that they forget they are thinkers, dreamers, visionaries in their own right. Kids, when asked to be creative thinkers, come up with marvelous ideas.

A vice-principal in a Miami junior high school tried unsuccessfully to solve the rowdy behavior in the seventh grade lunch hall. He called in a group of students, including some who were contributing to the disturbance and said, "How would you solve this problem?" The kids brainstormed a few minutes, then they said, "Have volunteer patrols of students monitoring the lunchroom. We listen best to kids our own age." The vice principal followed their plan and it worked beautifully.

We want to teach our youngsters to think, not just to process and evaluate other people's ideas, but to be creative thinkers in their own right. "What do *you* think? What would *you* do? What does that mean to *you*? Do *you* agree or disagree? What do *you* think *he* was thinking? What would happen if he was thinking differently?" When youngsters learn to see thought in operation behind every perception, every feeling and every behavior, when they learn to open their own mind to wisdom——to explore, discover and experiment with their own tool of thought without fear of ridicule or censure——we will have a renaissance, a new generation of informed, ingenious, inventive thinkers like we've not seen before.

These youngsters will know that thought is their most powerful, creative tool, that what they think has immediate, broad effect not only on their life, but on the life of every person with whom they come into contact.

These are the rewards of being an active participant in our thinking process:

- We feel in control of our lives, thinking from a full range of options.
- We recognize ourselves as the creative intelligence formulating the thoughts that become our perceptions, feelings and behaviors.
- We recognize and can choose to turn away from thinking patterns that diminish ourselves and others.

SUMMARY

Thought exists in two dimensions: (1) thought content, and (2) the ability to produce thought content. These two dimensions of thought enable us to work, not only with concepts, ideas, images, theories and philosophies, but with the levels of consciousness that formulates those things.

Our ability to think about thinking enables us to change ourselves by overcoming thought-created self-defeating tendencies. Break-the-mold classes, homes and counseling offices will be places where people learn not just *what* to think but *how* to think. They will be places where people examine intelligently the results of their thinking and how it influences their lives and the lives of those around them and, if the results are undesirable, to open their minds to the arising of new thought—to wisdom. Recognizing and working with two dimensions of thought will bring a renaissance in teaching and learning. As Pascal (1670)[1], observed, "Man is but a reed, but he is a thinking reed."

7

Lost

in Thought

There is nothing more damaging to human beings than thinking there is something wrong with them.

Human beings are born with enthusiasm, wisdom, creativity—gifts of every kind. So, why do we feel stuck, inadequate, insecure, unable to cope? The answer is thought. When potential is lost, it's lost in thought. Everything we achieve or fail to achieve is a result of our own thinking. Before we can use thought consistently for good, we have to understand its potential for harm.

AMY: A CASE OF MISPLACED MATH POTENTIAL

Amy, a bright-eyed second grader with tousled curls and a great sense of humor, missed three weeks of school, out with chicken pox. Amy was happy to resume classes, but her delight dissolved when her first math paper was handed back. There, at the top of the page, was a blazing red, double-underlined "U" for unsatisfactory. It was a shock. Until then, Amy made good grades without any problem. Looking at the "U," everything seemed different.

Preoccupied with the bad grade, Amy only half-heard the day's math lesson. Later, doing the assignment, she was confused, but too embarrassed to ask for help. When that paper came back, there was another "U" emblazoned on the top of the page. Next to it Mr. Adams had written, "See me." Before anyone saw her shame, Amy tore the paper into pieces and threw it in the wastebasket.

That afternoon her mother asked, "How are things going at school?" Amy said, "Fine," and ran outside to play before she was asked more questions. That night she dreamed of running through a dark, tangled forest, chased by The Giant U-Creature who was trying to eat her alive.

The next day, Amy was standing with a group of friends when she saw Mr. Adams walking toward her. She thought, "Oh, please, Mr. A, don't embarrass me in front of my friends," but Mr. Adams, not hearing her thoughts or seeing the anxious expression on her face, said, "Amy, what's going on? Did you take a dumb pill before math last week, or what? Pay attention in class, and if you have questions, ask me." Amy, counting the seconds until he went away, said, "Okay, Mr. Adams. I will," but she knew she couldn't face him.

Amy tried, but she was so worried about math, she couldn't think straight. Every "U" put her farther behind. Ashamed, Amy avoided Mr. Adams and found excuses not to talk to him. Eventually, Amy got so used to seeing "U" on her math papers she expected it. She gave up trying to be a good math student, stopped paying attention in class and at test time, guessing at answers, marking anything that seemed halfway plausible, Amy was the first one to hand in her paper. Now, thinking math comprehension was beyond her, Amy lived in a math-disabled reality. This reality wasn't based on fact, because Amy could understand mathematics as well as any other student her age. Her reality was a product of self-defeating thoughts that ended in a self-fulfilling prophecy. Here's how it worked.

Amy's thought, "I can't do math," produced feelings of shame, anxiety and frustration. These feelings clouded her mind, blocked her natural intelligence and discouraged her, so she gave up without trying. Every time Amy got a poor grade she'd think, "This proves it. I can't do math," and the cycle was confirmed and strengthened. This cycle is shown in Figure 7-1.

Figure 7-1
Amy's Thought-Created Cycle of Disability

THOUGHT
"I can't do math."

RESULT   FEELINGS
Mental Blocks   Shame, Anxiety,
Poor Grades   Inadequacy, Frustration

BEHAVIOR
Giving Up, Avoidance

Unaware that Amy's poor performance was thought-related, Mr. Adams came to think of Amy as a poor student, one lacking mathematical aptitude. Accepting this thought as a fact, Mr. Adams changed his behavior toward Amy. He expected good work from the other students, but not from her. He searched her papers, not for correct answers, but for errors which he highlighted and underscored in red. When Amy's work showed promise, as it sometimes did, Mr. Adams discounted it as a fluke, a stroke of luck. He assumed that somebody else did it or that Amy copied the work. Now, Mr. Adams would never think of encouraging Amy in math for fear of arousing "false hope." Mr. Adam's thinking created his own self-fulfilling, prophecy of disabling thought, feelings and behavior. This cycle is illustrated in Figure 7-2.

Figure 7-2
Mr. Adam's Thought-Created Cycle of Disability

THOUGHT
"Amy can't do math."

RESULT
Amy gets poor grades

FEELINGS
Resignation, Helplessness

BEHAVIOR
Giving Up, Avoidance

Eventually, the school psychologist was asked to evaluate Amy's mathematical aptitude, and, not surprisingly, Amy scored low on all tests. At the faculty staffing it was unanimous, "Amy has a math disability."

Amy's parents were given the bad news and shown stacks of papers marked in red. They are advised to place Amy in a special math program for disabled students, but told, "Don't worry. Lots of girls have trouble with math. She can take home economics and typing in high school, marry the captain of the football team and raise beautiful children."

Amy's parents were devastated, but they trustingly accepted the educators' evaluation. Before the week was over, aunts, uncles, grandparents, second cousins twice removed and the grocer down the street all knew that Amy, a good person in many ways, just couldn't compute. Cousin Harriet, from Jersey, announced at Thanksgiving dinner that Aunt Millie on her father's side had trouble with math, and everyone agreed: Amy's disability is genetic. She'd inherited a recessive math gene. Uncle Cal advised Amy to marry a man who could balance her checkbook.

In and out of the classroom, Mr. Adams talked freely of Amy's math impairment and his thoughts about Amy, which were now confirmed beliefs accepted by the other teachers. Amy's next-year's teacher had already planned to put her in the remedial group. The kids in Amy's school also knew the score. Amy's classmates nominated her for class secretary but not for treasurer. They'll elected her Prom Queen but they didn't trust her to buy the decorations.

So we see how an insecure thought that began in the mind of a little girl grew into a consensually accepted feedback cycle of disability, complete with academic, psychological and genetic validation. Math ineptitude became a fixed part of Amy's self-concept. Of course it wasn't part of Amy's actual identity because she was fully capable of understanding mathematics; but it was how she learned to think about herself and her options for the future. Once Amy "learned" that she couldn't do math and that learning became a fixed part of her thinking, all Amy's future math moments, based on a false premise, became unteachable.

Mr. Adams, accepting false, limiting beliefs but not knowing it, struggled with teaching. He worked hard, but he was always frustrated by the number of students who failed to learn as they should. He said, "They have the IQ's for it, but they just can't do it. I don't know what's wrong with today's kids, they just don't apply themselves," never knowing that the missing link between potential and performance is thought. Fortunately, this isn't the case with Mr. David, a teacher who sees the connection between thought and behavior.

MISTY: FROM FAILURE TO SUCCESS

The first week of school, Misty sat by herself crying. Mr. David, the first grade teacher, sat beside her and asked, "What's the matter?" Misty's brown eyes rimmed with tears, "I can't read," she said quietly. Mr. David looked into her sad eyes and said, "Of course you can't read, Misty. That's why you came to first grade, to learn to read." "No, you don't understand." Misty replied. "I *can't* read. Everyone else in kindergarten could read. I can't." Worry and shame clouded her young face. Mr. David realized that

Misty, barely six years old, had a problem, not a reading problem, but a thought problem.

Mr. David said, "Misty, listen to me carefully. You only *think* you can't read. That thought isn't true. Believe me. You *can* read. I'll teach you how. Reading is not only easy, it's fun. Here, let me show you." Mr. David grabbed a sheet of paper and printed a three-line phonetic story titled, "The Fat Cat." He illustrated it with a picture of an overnourished kitty that made Misty smile. Mr. David laughed and said, "I know. It's a good thing I'm a teacher and not an artist."

Mr. David said, "Misty, I'm going to read this story a couple of times. You watch the words while I read, then later I will prove how easy it is to read." Mr. David read the story three times. Then he said, "Now, Misty. You do it." Misty teared up. "I can't read, Mr. David," she said. Mr. David smiled, "Okay, I'll tell you what. You start reading and whenever you need help, I'll whisper in your ear. Between the two of us, we'll get this job done."

Misty began reading. When she stumbled on a word, Mr. David told her what it was and she continued. At the end of the story, she gulped in relief. Mr. David looked at her seriously and felt her forehead. "It was a close call, but I think you are going to live. Let's do it again."

Several more times they read the story; each time Misty read more confidently than before. Then, on the fifth try, Misty read the story perfectly. Mr. David looked into her eyes and said, "Misty, you are reading. Do it again."

Like a starving girl eating bread, Misty read the story again and again. She read it to John and Harriet, to Bill and Joe, Susan, Marty and Jim. Shining with pride, Misty read the story to the school secretary, the librarian and the principal. She called home and read it to her mother over the phone.

That afternoon, standing in line for the school bus, Misty threw her arms around Mr. David and said, "You, my beautiful teacher, you taught me to read." Mr. David smiled. Misty was already thinking of herself as a reader. The battle was won. From now on, all her reading moments would be teachable.

At the first parent-teacher conference, Misty's parents were apprehensive. They confessed their meetings with Misty's kindergarten teacher had been a disaster. The first time they met this teacher, she had announced sternly, Misty can't read. She's only memorizing words. I'm afraid this is quite a serious problem. Are you giving Misty attention at home? Does she have responsibilities around the house? Perhaps you should have another child so Misty doesn't grow up an only child, spoiled and self-centered. You know, a teacher can't make up at school for what a child misses at home."

Misty's parents left the conferences believing their daughter had a learning problem that was probably their fault, but without the slightest idea how to help her. At the end of the year, against the kindergarten teacher's judgment, Misty's parents insisted she be passed to first grade. All summer they agonized, hoping they'd made the right decision.

When Mr. David heard this story, he said, "You have nothing to worry about. In the early stages of reading a student should be memorizing words. This is actually an excellent sign, one we would hope to see. I advise you to drop the thought that Misty can't read. That will get in her way more than anything else. Believe me. Your daughter is bright and capable and doing well in reading. I'm delighted with her progress."

Misty's parents, tears in their eyes, asked, "How can we help?" Mr. David said, "Love your daughter. Believe in her with all your heart. Enjoy her company. Provide a happy, peaceful home where she can relax and unwind after a busy day and refresh herself for the next day's challenges. Read her good stories and when she feels ready, listen to her read. That's your job. That's what you do best. My job is to teach Misty to read. That's what I do best." Misty's parents left the conference strengthened, fortified with new, more factual thoughts, ones that would bring out the best in themselves and in their daughter.

CREATING UNTEACHABLE MOMENTS

There is nothing more damaging to human beings than learning to think something is wrong with them. Nothing limits a person more than learning to think he is a failure. When people think this way, their moments become unteachable. This is why retention rarely helps. If, by being held back a grade, a youngster learns to think there is something wrong with his ability to learn, and this is how retention is usually perceived by youngsters, then all his future moments will be unteachable——or only minimally teachable——because his mind will be closed to the possibility of excellent, joyful learning. To create teachable moments, we must protect youngsters from learning to think that there is something wrong with their ability to learn. We must protect youngsters from this destructive thinking with the same vigor as we protect them from smallpox.

This is not to say we don't allow people to explore, to dare, to take risks or to experience the consequences of their actions, for making mistakes and learning from them——trial and error——is an important part of the learning process. But it's deadly to equate mistakes with failure because if we do, we will pass this thinking on to our students, clients and youngsters and it will stop them.

Most of us have learned to associate mistakes with failure. It's our conditioning, the way we were taught to think. The first step in creating teachable moments for ourselves and others is to break consciously from this and other faulty, limiting thinking we've unconsciously accepted in the past.

TO LABEL IS TO PROGRAM FAILURE

To create teachable moments, we must stop programming people for failure by lumping their weakest qualities together and assigning a label to it, such as "learning disabled," "overachiever," "underachiever," "discipline problem," "mentally disabled," "severely emotionally disturbed," "troublemaker," "liar," "thief," and so on. Labels, more than describing limitations, become limitations in their own right. Labels become mental hooks on which people hang their thoughts about disability and failure.

Assigning labels to people, we condition them and ourselves to think there is something wrong with them. Labels are nothing more than thoughts that, if accepted, stop human potential in its tracks. As long as we assign weakness-centered labels to students, we will suffer the consequences of our own self-fulfilling prophecies.

Tom: The Emotionally Disturbed Teenager

Tom's parents took him to a psychologist because he was misbehaving, skipping school and flunking his classes. When the psychologist called Tom and his parents into his office, he announced, "My tests show that Tom is emotionally disturbed. He needs extensive, ongoing therapy and possibly a special school program." Tom and his parents, accepting this label of irreversible emotional damage, were devastated. They left the psychologist's office feeling they'd been given a psychological death warrant.

Thinking of Tom as "disturbed," his parents began to see signs of emotional instability in everything he did. When Tom was early for dinner, he was obsessive compulsive. When he was late, he was resisting authority. If he was on time, he was overcompensating, trying too hard to please.

Thinking of himself as defective, Tom stopped holding himself responsible for healthy feelings and behavior. He no longer resisted feelings of discouragement but gave in to depression. He stopped going to school and seeing his friends. He stayed in his dark room and listened to gloomy music all day, eventually refusing to come out, even for meals. Tom, thinking, feeling and behaving as if he were emotionally damaged, became a perfect fit for the mentally disturbed profile.

Watching Tom's condition worsen, his desperate parents took him to another psychologist. Fortunately, this professional differed from the first in two significant ways:

1. he believed people were born with the capability and disposition for healthy functioning, and
2. he knew that dysfunctional realities were created and maintained by dysfunctional thinking.

Interviewing Tom from this frame of reference, this psychologist came to a different conclusion. Talking to Tom and his parents, this psychologist said, "I have good news. Tom is a normal fourteen-year-old boy going through the insecure thoughts and confusing mood swings that are common at adolescence. I predict that after Tom learns how to handle his thoughts and moods more effectively, he will be just fine."

Everyone wept in relief. In the weeks that followed, Tom and his parents learned to recognize and disengage from negative thinking patterns and the low moods that came with them. Thinking of Tom as a normal adolescent, his parents no longer saw his punctuality——or lack of it——as a sign of mental instability, but the normal behavior of a fourteen-year-old. They could deal with that.

Tom later told the counselor, "When I thought there was something wrong with me, I started acting like it and I got worse. Now that I feel normal again, I'm acting normal again and you can't imagine how good it feels." Tom went back to school and his grades improved. He told the counselor, "Teachers are actually stopping me in the hall to say how much I've improved. It's great. But best of all, I dropped the thoughts that were making me too scared to get to know girls. Guess what. Girls love me. They think I'm a stud!"

Several months after Tom stopped seeing the counselor, the counselor got this note from Tom's mother.

How can we thank you? Now that we look for health instead of illness, the change in Tom is unbelievable. He goes to school without a fight, does his assignments and his grades have skyrocketed. He's got friends and talks on the phone for hours just like other teenagers. It's so nice to hear laughter in the house again. Thank you.

Tom's "emotionally disturbed" label became a self-fulfilling prophecy. When Tom and his parents "learned" that he was mentally ill and accepted this idea into their thinking, then Tom's future moments became unteachable, closed to mental health. Later, when they learned that he was mentally healthy and accepted this idea into their thinking, Tom's moments were teachable, open to mental health.

When a parent tells his daughter, "You are a troublemaker," he is giving that girl a dysfunctional way to think about herself, one that, if she accepts it, closes her mind to other options. Negative classifications, if accepted, become faulty beliefs. Faulty beliefs, habitually acted out, give the affected person no relief or chance for change.

A human being is too full of possibilities to be defined by a label. If someone labels you or your student, client or youngster, don't let the label become part of the way you think, feel and behave. Open your mind to the wisdom inside and take another look. Looking through loving, unbiased eyes, you will see the health that has always been there just waiting for an invitation to come out. Then you will discover more truly who you really are, or who your children or clients or students really are.

Without self-defeating thoughts blocking their way, people accomplish the unbelievable. People with low IQ's learn to read, write and compute. People without sight water-ski, golf and ice skate. People without legs play basketball and climb mountains. Without self-defeating thoughts to hold them back, "emotionally disturbed" people become happy, healthy and successful.

After I'd done a training workshop in Chicago, a teacher handed me a note. It said,

> *All the water in the seven seas cannot sink a ship, unless the water gets inside. All the bad thoughts in the world cannot hurt you, unless you accept them into consciousness.*

When you understand how unconsciously accepted, self-limiting thoughts create unteachable moments, you are careful what thoughts you keep in your consciousness. Keeping your mind open to possibilities doesn't mean forcing good thoughts. It means letting wisdom inspire you with thoughts not yet created.

SUMMARY

Whatever we think, and believe, becomes our personal experience. Dysfunctional beliefs block potential and create unteachable moments. If you don't know dysfunction is belief-based, you waste your time trying to fix the problems that result from faulty thinking rather than fixing the thinking itself. You wear yourself out bailing water instead of plugging the hole.

Understanding the connection between potential and thought, you open your thought to possibilities and find yourself and those you care about, living in wisdom, beyond belief.

8

Unrecognized Beliefs

Can Cripple Your Potential

Everything we achieve or fail to achieve is a result of what we believe.

Mental health, wisdom and self-esteem are natural states that are blocked by self-limiting beliefs that we accept as facts. Positive beliefs release more capability than negative ones, but every belief, even constructive ones, carries certain limits and conditions. Understanding how beliefs block potential frees us from creating a lifetime of unteachable moments for ourselves and others.

MRS. GEORGE AND THE GENIUSES

Mrs. George examined the roster of students for the coming year. "Look at those IQ scores," she thought, "For the first time in twenty-two years, I've been assigned a class of intellectually gifted students. This is going to be a great year!"

The year flew by and all the students did exceptionally well. They had their rough times, of course, Mrs. George expected that, but she knew that each set-back was just a phase, that no matter how bad it looked, each student had the innate ability for academic success. It was an outstanding year.

Before leaving for the summer, Mrs. George stopped by the principal's office, "I want to thank you for assigning me such a talented group of youngsters this year. I only wish I had kids like that every year." The principal looked puzzled, "I don't know what you mean," she said. Mrs. George responded, "All my students had high IQ scores. Here it is right here." The teacher handed the principal the class registration with the numbers beside each student's name. The principal looked at the list and said, "You're not going to believe this, Diane, but those numbers aren't IQ scores. They're locker numbers."

Mrs. George's students were no brighter this year than they were any other year, but she believed they were, and that belief created a year of exceptionally teachable moments. A teacher's beliefs affects student achievement. Research in this area is fascinating.

THE CASE OF THE LATE BLOOMERS

In one well-known study, Rosenthal and Jacobson (1968)[1] tested classrooms of elementary students. Then, *at random*, they picked a few students out of each class and told the teachers that these particular students had been identified as "late bloomers." A "late bloomer" was a student who, regardless of past performance, would make a significant gain in achievement this year. At the end of the year, all the students were retested. Surprisingly, those students whom the teachers expected to "bloom," this year had actually learned more than their classmates!

Another researcher, Page (1958)[2], divided his class arbitrarily into Group A, Group B and Group C. He taught all three groups the same, with one difference. He devised differing ways to communicate his expectations to his students. On Group A papers, Page put only a grade. On Group B papers, he put a grade and added an encouraging word, such as, "good," "well done," or "excellent." On Group C papers, Page not only put a grade but he wrote a narrative making it clear he'd read the paper carefully, knew what was in it and appreciated the aspects of it that were good.

Later, Page did a statistical study comparing the achievement of the three groups. The results were startling. Group A's and Group B's achievement were about the same. However, Group C students, the ones who received evidence of the teacher's positive expectations, all showed *a statistically significant gain in achievement*. All ended up fulfilling or surpassing teacher expectations!

How does teacher expectation affect student performance? Good and Brophy (1975)[3] describe a five-step process.

1. The teacher expects specific behavior and achievement from particular students.
2. Because of these expectations, the teacher behaves differently toward different students.
3. This treatment by the teacher tells each student what behavior he or she expects. This treatment affects the student's self-concept, achievement, motivation and level of aspiration.
4. If the teacher's behavior is consistent over time and if the student does not actively resist or change in the some way, the teacher expectation will shape student behavior in a certain way. High expectation students will be led to achieve at high levels but the achievement of low-expectation students will decline.
5. With time, student achievement and behavior will conform more closely to that expected.

Youngsters achieve what they expect to achieve. Usually, they expect to achieve what is expected of them.

STAND AND DELIVER

The book, *Escalante: The Best Teacher In America*[4], which was made into the movie, *Stand And Deliver*, tells the remarkable story of what happened when a teacher, Jamie Escalante, believed that a group of minority kids from the East Los Angeles barrio could learn advanced calculus.

Eighteen of Escalante's Hispanic students were accused of cheating on an advanced placement calculus test by the Educational Testing Service in Princeton, New Jersey. How, the testing board asked, could this group of minority kids from a school known for vandalism, gang violence, a drop out rate of fifty-five percent, and the lowest math scores in the nation, pass a test so difficult that fewer than two percent of American high school students even attempt it?

Yet, when these students took the test again, they passed it a second time. The reason? Their teacher, Jamie Escalante, refused to accept the years of accumulated, consensual beliefs about these kids, beliefs held by the principal, the other teachers, the math department, the parents, the students themselves and the testing service, that these kids couldn't possibly master advanced calculus.

Inspired by his unwavering belief in these kids' ability to learn calculus, Escalante used his own unique methods to break students out of their failure-oriented thinking patterns. He posted signs such as, "Calculus Need Not Be Made Easy. It Is Easy Already." He challenged, goaded, cajoled, and teased——anything he could think of——to get his students to open their minds. It wasn't easy. It took time, but Escalante refused to give up and eventually, his students began living up to his expectations.

Once the kids started learning, they started coming to school at 7 A.M. for extra study! That first year, eighteen students passed the advanced placement test, not only once, but twice! The next year, 1983, thirty out of thirty-three students passed the test. In 1984, 122 students took the test and ninety-three percent passed it.

People try to duplicate Mr. Escalante's results by copying his techniques, but his power is not in the techniques he uses. Escalante's power is his unwavering belief in his students' ability, not only to learn, but to *excel*. If you sincerely believe in a person's ability, any technique, method or curriculum comes alive in your hands. A teacher, counselor or parent whose beliefs support ability, will use their own techniques, perhaps ones quite different from Escalante's, but whatever they do will achieve excellent results. However, if your belief supports disability, if you think people are limited and can only accomplish so much, the best techniques in the world can't take you or your students beyond that belief.

A drunk walked into a stop sign. Dazed and confused, he stepped back, brushed himself off and advanced in the same direction, only to run headlong into the stop sign again. He retreated, waited, then with renewed determination, marched forward again, only to collide again with the sign. After he'd done this several times, he threw his arms in the air and said, "It's no use. I'm surrounded, stopped everywhere I turn." This is our predicament holding onto limiting beliefs. We're surrounded, stopped everywhere we turn.

ABOUT BELIEFS

When we think about beliefs, we usually think of our most cherished standards or religious convictions, those tenets that we have consciously chosen. Most Americans believe in life, liberty and the pursuit of happiness. Most of all we believe in the right to believe whatever we want to believe. We know we have these beliefs because we went through a process of evaluation and selection to choose them. This is how it should be. However, for every belief we have consciously chosen, we have hundreds more that are and unconsciously adopted, hidden, yet deeply ingrained in our thought patterns. Unconsciously adopted beliefs are the ones that produce dysfunctional results. Commonly held, disabling beliefs are:

- I (You) can't do it. I'm (you're) not up to it.
- I'm (You're) not enough. I'm (you're) not perfect. There's something I (you) lack.
- Teaching/learning must be a struggle.
- People must treat me a certain way or I can't be happy.
- No pain, no gain.
- That will never work.
- I (you) will let people down (or look foolish or get hurt).
- I (you) must have this to be happy (or successful or good).
- I'm (you're) too old to change.
- I (you) must do well.
- When I don't live up to my own or other people's expectations, I'm a bad person.
- I have limitations I can never overcome.
- Change must be difficult.

- People who don't meet my expectations are bad and deserve to be punished.

An Open Mind: A Terrible Thing to Lose

An activated belief system doesn't let new things in. It screens them out.

We're not talking about opinions or preferences. What we're talking about goes much deeper than whether we prefer Chevys or Fords. The beliefs we're talking about are so deeply ingrained they don't look like thoughts, they look like life! Beliefs are our deepest, most basic ideas *about what's true* about ourselves and other people. A deeply ingrained idea about what's true about ourselves and other people is insidious because if something doesn't fit with it, we automatically refute it, modify it, discard it, refuse to consider it, or don't even see it at all. An activated belief system does not question the validity of its own conclusions. In an active belief system, the test of validity for an idea is whether we already agree with it.

History is full of examples of closed belief systems in action. Marco Polo returned from China eager to share his discoveries about a new world, but he was thrown into prison for talking about a place his countrymen didn't believe existed! Galileo was imprisoned, his life threatened for saying that the earth was not the center of the universe. The first physician to introduce the idea of painless surgery was laughed out of the operating theater because at that time patients' screams were considered to be a necessary part of the surgical process. Lister was ridiculed by his medical colleagues for washing his hands before surgery. He was condemned for having postoperative patients with clean wounds because medical thinking of the day believed that inflammation and infection were signs of healing. Introducing a new idea into a fixed belief system is not for the fainthearted.

It takes courage to reexamine our beliefs, to let outdated or dysfunctional ideas collapse. Picasso remarked that every act of creation was first an act of destruction. Before we can create a new, better reality for ourselves and others, some of our favorite longheld, self-limiting beliefs have to be set free. Once we have a belief, even one that does not serve us well, we tend to hold on to it. When we do suspend our beliefs about who we are and what is possible for us, about our youngsters and what is possible for them, then we step——literally——beyond belief. Beyond belief is the space where miracles happen.

Beliefs and Behavior

Behavior is belief made visible. We do what we do because of what we believe. Mr. Adams treated Amy as a poor math risk because he believed she was one. Misty behaved like a nonreader because she believed she couldn't read. Mrs. George treated her class like genuises because that's what she believed they were. If you want to know what you believe, watch how you behave. Behavior is belief taking form. Beliefs not only affect our own behavior, they also affect the way other people behave around us.

One teacher's beliefs make her confident, capable and decisive. She expects the highest in achievement, productivity and behavior from her students and she gets it. But the teacher across the hall has beliefs that make her insecure, tentative, afraid to expect the best, and in her classroom these same students don't do as well. Parents whose beliefs prevent them from setting high standards and enforcing limits have kids that get away with murder at home. Those same kids behave like angels with a baby-sitter who has beliefs that enable her to set firm limits and hold youngsters accountable for their actions.

Think of someone who holds a negative belief of you. How do you behave with this person? What comes out, your best or your worst? Around people who expect you to bungle, you bungle. It's frustrating. No matter what you do, you can't seem to do anything right. But around people who trust you to do the best and give you a nonjudgmental hand up over the hard places, you shine. Because of what they believe, people:

- scold a clumsy child, making him more awkward;
- badger a poor reader, making him a worse reader;

- nag a slow learner, making her a slower learner; or
- attack a resistant client, making him more oppositional.

Parents who believe in their children's ability for common sense, clear thinking and responsible behavior bring out the best in their youngsters, whatever the particular child-rearing philosophy they practice. On the other hand, parents who believe youngsters are weak, inadequate or unlovable raise children who feel insecure and unworthy. It doesn't matter what child-rearing techniques they use. Counselors who believe in their client's ability for healthy change behave in ways that strengthen this tendency in their clients regardless of the counseling theory they follow. Counselors who believe people can't rise above disability and dysfunction behave in ways that set these conditions in their clients, regardless of their therapy orientation. What a person believes, and how they behave as a result of it, is more important and influential than the techniques they use.

We run into problems because of the way we think. A youngster with an IQ of 85 learned to walk and talk and a hundred other amazing things before they came to school, but in school that child's parents will *not* be told:

Your youngster has his own unique talent and special genius. Love him. Believe in him. Let him spread his wings and find out who he is. Who knows where his heart and spirit will take him with your support. Encourage him, enjoy him. He's a natural!

No, this child and his parents will be bombarded verbally and nonverbally by beliefs that entrap the emerging spirit in caution and gloom. Such beliefs lead teachers to say:

IQ-85's are limited. They may be nice people, but they don't do very well and they don't go very far. Don't get your hopes up. Expect the worst and you won't be disappointed.

But as a baby, little "IQ-85" and his parents had no beliefs that he'd better not try to walk because it might be too much for him. They had no beliefs that it was "false hope" to assume he could learn speech and language like little "IQ-120" down the street. So little "IQ-85," with no limiting beliefs to hold him back, accomplished the impossible and enjoyed doing it. Preschool children express what seems like unusual genius because they have not yet accepted beliefs that hold them back from doing and being their best.

Beliefs and Reality

Whatever we believe becomes real for us, even if it isn't real to anyone else. If I believe in a shortage of time, I'll never have enough time. If I believe learning is hard, I'll struggle with it. If I believe administrators can't be trusted, I'll never meet an administrator I can trust. If I believe a knot in my stomach proves I'm a caring, responsible person, I obligate myself to stomach cramps. If I believe love equals worry, when I love, I must worry. If I believe people don't like me, I'll behave in ways that eventually pushes them away. Then I'll say, "I knew it. People just don't like me."

The influence of beliefs on teaching and learning cannot be overestimated. If I believe I'm slow or damaged, this belief makes learning incredibly difficult. If I believe I have the capability to function in a wholesome way, this belief frees and strengthens my ability. Through our beliefs, we get exactly what we expect.

THE WAY OUT

What is a teacher, parent or counselor's first line of defense against unrecognized potential-freezing beliefs that we don't even know that we have? Our protection is twofold. First, be aware that you have unrecognized self-limiting beliefs. Two, look for the disabling feelings they produce.

As you go through your day, stay awake for thoughts that sap your energy, close you off and shut you down, thoughts that say,

"Forget it. Give up. Nothing's going to change. Nothing warm and nourishing can happen here." The tragedy of unrecognized, "It's hopeless to hope," thoughts is that they cut us off from our most inspired thinking and most supportive feelings. Such thoughts come in hundreds of forms. Some of the most common are:

"What's the use?"
"It's hopeless."
"No one understands."
"This is too much."
"I've tried too hard."
"I'll never get through this."
"This is the best I (he, she or they) can do."

Sometimes you catch negative thought in action. Usually, you don't catch the thought itself, but key into the feeling it leaves behind. You can't mistake the emotional results of negative thinking, those dismal, push-away feelings of apathy, resignation, frustration, anger, insecurity and hopelessness. When you lose your perspective and your sense of humor, when things look impossible, irreversibly desperate and you feel serious, discouraged, jaded, stuck, you can bet the farm, you've just been backsided by your own mental framework, trapped in your own adverse thought structure!

When a thinker wakes up to the emotional and/or behavioral results of their negative thinking, an instant transformation takes place. We pull back, disengage, take a deep breath and wait for the muddy water to clear. When the water is clear, the next step is obvious, simple, common sense.

But be careful. Don't be tempted to cloud the water even more by substituting a good belief for a bad one, a happy thought for a sad one. Don't try to fool yourself by playing, "Let's pretend I don't think that. Let's pretend I think something else." This kind of self-deception doesn't work. You're too intelligent for that.

There's a story about a Zen Master who told a student, "Go out back where no one is looking and kill a chicken for dinner." Hours later the student returned empty handed. He said, "I'm sorry Master, but everywhere I went, the chicken could always see." When you try to trick yourself by substituting one belief for another it doesn't work because you can always see.

You don't live beyond belief by substituting a new limit for an old one. A woman believes, "I can't be happy in this situation." Then realizing her predicament, she opens a hairline crack in hope by substituting the thought, "I can't be happy but I can learn to cope with my unhappiness." She's still not free. She's still focusing on unhappiness. To get free, this woman has to open her mind so wide she sees that her belief in perpetual misery is a mental illusion.

A hypnotized person thinks he's a chicken, but once the mesmerism is broken, he doesn't have to substitute the new belief, "I am a human being," for the old one, "I am a barnyard fowl." The minute the mental spell is broken, this man knows the truth and now he thinks, feels and behaves like a human being instead of a Rhode Island Red. It sounds easy and it is, except we are so identified with what we think, we resist letting go. We'd love to change, but not at the expense of what we think.

Once we see a false belief as thought-created and maintained, we don't have to fight it, fear it or substitute something else for it. If you look at a rope and think it's a snake, the way out is *not* to panic, to stock up on snake-bite kits or join a Fear-of-Reptiles support group. These things only make sense if you're really dealing with snakes. The minute you open your thought, take a deeper look and see you are dealing with ropes, not reptiles, you're home free. But, you may wonder, what if what I'm seeing really is a snake? Consider this story.

Loving The Hand That Bites You

Rick, hearing the screech of brakes, ran into the street to find his dog lying in the middle of the street, hit by a car. When Rick tried to help the wounded animal, it bit his hand and drew blood. What did Rick see? A vicious, stupid animal attacking someone who loved him and was only trying to help? Did Rick get his feelings hurt and say, "Bad dog, Shame on you. You don't deserve my help." No, of course not. Rick, seeing the hurt and fear behind the lashing out, was filled with compassion. He loved his dog more than ever.

What did Rick see? A rope or a snake? If you know that people as well as animals lash out when they are hurt and that you can guage the degree of hurt by the degree of the lashing out, you can help, protected by your understanding of the source of their push-away behavior. We never err on the side of compassion.

Reality is an elusive thing. You see something that is true at one level, then you look again and see a deeper truth.

Michael: Changed Belief, Changed Life

Michael was one of those kids who drives teachers crazy. He interrupted, acted silly, talked back, complained and made a hundred excuses for not doing his work. Later, as a clinical psychologist, Michael recalled the teacher that changed his life.

My smart-aleck behavior was a cover-up. With English as a second language, I believed I couldn't do the work, and terrified someone would find out. Afraid of looking dumb, I didn't ask questions or go for help. I acted as if good behavior was beneath me; I pretended I didn't care about school or good grades. Teachers hated me and I hated them. I lived for the day I could drop out of school. Then in seventh grade, I met a teacher who was different.

Miss Chung saw through the repulsive, push-away behavior to the scared kid hiding underneath. Quietly, she took me under her wing, asked me to stay after school to help her, and we talked. Miss Chung never said, "Michael, there's more to you than you think. You're in for some pleasant surprises," but I felt it when I was around her. She saw something in me I couldn't see myself. It was puzzling but I liked it.

Miss Chung worked with me, encouraged me, humored me, laughed with me, challenged and helped me until I understood the concepts. She never made me feel dumb. Even when it took me a long time to understand, she was always there, pulling for me, on my side, knowing I'd eventually get it. That semester, I got my first 'A'. That was the year I fell in love, with Miss Chung, with school and most of all, with learning.

Miss Chung didn't try to talk Michael out of his negative beliefs. You can't argue people out of dysfunctional beliefs. Beliefs, whatever they are, are internally consistent and externally validated. She didn't attack Michael's beliefs head on, she created an experience where Michael's wisdom could come to the fore and he could see himself differently. She showed, not told, a better way.

When All You've Got Isn't Enough

When you say to your most difficult student, "Good morning. I'm happy to see you today," and you get back, "Save your happy-crap for someone who cares," it takes lots of wisdom to see the hurt behind the lashing out; to have the understanding and the dedication not to give up.

No matter what you do, some people won't be ready to give up their beliefs. They've been so wounded, their hurts take longer to heal. No matter what you do, some people will close the door and block you out. Do the best you can. Call on all the wisdom and love you've got, knowing if you can't help this person, perhaps at another time someone else can. Smile and go on. It's not your job to save the whole world. It is your job to do the best you can and preserve your strength and mental health for those who are ready. Give the best you've got, believe in change with all your heart, but don't be attached to the outcome.

Having a Choice

Knowing what beliefs are and how they work, we have choice. Realizing we are the thinker, the one making up the whole thing to suit ourselves, we can follow an activated belief system or step outside for a new look. For a new look, we quiet compulsive thinking, open thought and let wisdom show glimmers of new possibilities.

SUMMARY

The ultimate tyranny over the minds of human beings is self-limiting beliefs they don't know they have. Understanding how thinkers inadvertently bring *dis*ability to life through thought frees us from limitation.

The human mind is vast, limitless. We have potential beyond our dreams. We must never underestimate the ability of the human mind and spirit to rise above grim forecasts. We start by opening our minds.

I am up to this. I can do it. I am enough. I'm not perfect, but I am enough.

9

Automatic Thought . . .

Help or Hinderance?

Our brain, our biological computer, doesn't know which way is up until we tell it, and we can tell it anything we want.

Harry, a gregarious, competent man who's been teaching ninth grade for fifteen years, is walking to class when Mrs. Black, the principal, walks by him in the hall. Harry says a cheerful, "Good morning," but the administrator passes without saying a word. Suddenly, Harry's well-being is replaced with feelings of insecurity and dread. What changed Harry's feelings? The answer is simple: Harry, without knowing it, is responding to his own thought.

How can an intelligent man respond to his own thought and not know it? It's not as strange as it seems. When Harry thinks about thinking, he considers thought that is consciously called and directed. However, the thought that disturbed Harry wasn't premeditated or deliberate. Harry didn't ask for it and he didn't see it coming. This thought was triggered, not by Harry's intention, but by Mrs. Black's silence. There are two forms of thought.

1. Consciously called and directed thinking
2. Automatically triggered cognition

CONSCIOUSLY DIRECTED THINKING

Consciously called and directed thinking is what we bring into play when someone asks, "Where shall we eat? Chinese or Greek?" You stop, consider, compare, contrast, reflect and make a decision. You know you are thinking because you witness thought in action.

Using consciously called and directed thought we analyze, evaluate, guess, recall, explore, consider, choose and decide. This form of thought enables us to recite The Periodic Table of Elements at family functions, convert miles to kilometers, differentiate an esophagus from a pharynx, plan a talk for Rotary, find our way around a new city, remember mother's birthday or recall the name of the person we've just met. Consciously directed thought is easy to identify: we know we're thinking because we watch ourselves doing it. This isn't the case with automatically triggered cognition.

AUTOMATICALLY ACTIVATED COGNITION

Automatically activated thought triggered from memory is different from insight, which has its source in our deeper wisdom or common sense. Insight, discussed in the next chapter, is the source of new thought, a fresh idea or realization, something you've never seen quite that way before. Thought triggered from memory, is not new thought, but old, based on our learning in the past.

When Harry was a boy, his mother was silent when she was angry so, over time, Harry came to associate silent women with anger. Pavlov's dogs, given food as a bell was rung, became conditioned to salivate at the sound of a bell even in the absence of food. Harry, learning to associate silence with anger became conditioned to feel upset around quiet women, even in the absence of anger.

Conditioning: Mental Associations

The human mind can pair any event with any other in terms of cause and effect, even when no such relationship exists. Our brain ——our biological computer——doesn't know which way is up until we tell it, and we can tell it anything we want. Max makes a hole-in-one wearing his Hawaiian print shirt and now, associating the shirt with good fortune, he won't wear any other shirt on the green. Samantha enjoys popcorn Monday night watching *Mash* reruns and next Monday when the program comes on, she has an inexplicable urge for Redenbacher's. This "urge" is the associative thought, "Mash equals popcorn," triggered by the program. If Samantha eats popcorn the second night, the association between *Mash* and popcorn will be strengthened and the following Monday the "urge" for Redenbacher's will be even stronger.

Advertising campaigns are built around our ability to make mental associations. Beer commercials pair drinking with having fun, knowing that people watching will make an unconscious mental association between alcohol and having a good time. It works. Cigarette advertisements pair smoking with sex-appeal. Viewers, not knowing how conditioning works, buy cigarettes to be more attractive to the opposite sex and, in their quest for sex appeal, become addicted to nicotine.

Automatically activated memory brings the past into the present. If you had carnations in your yard when you were eight-years-old, when you're forty the smell of carnations can make you feel like a kid again. If a bee from one of those carnations stung you on the nose, you may, today, feel unaccountably squeamish in the carnation section of a florist shop. When Charlotte was a child, her father hit her when he was angry. Now, as a woman, Charlotte feels insecure around irritated men. A Persian proverb says, "He who has been bitten by a snake, fears a piece of string." It's conditioning.

Harry's past has conditioned him to associate quiet woman with anger. When Mrs. Black walked by without speaking, Harry's automatic thought was, "She's mad at me." This triggered mental association didn't seem like a thought; it seemed to be an observation or perception that originated in the situation. If you asked Harry, "What makes you think Mrs. Black is angry," he would say, "I don't *think* she's mad at me. I *know* she is. I have eyes. I can see. The woman's obviously furious." Harry, so sure his perception is the only possibility that exists, closes his mind to other options.

Later, when Harry sees Mrs. Black in the lunchroom, she smiles and says, "You look nice today Harry. Is that a new tie?"

Harry, still stinging from his earlier upset, snaps, "I may not succeed, but I try to look presentable every day." Mrs. Black, startled by Harry's heated response, excuses herself to tend to other duties. As she walks away, Harry thinks, "I knew it. She *is* mad," and Harry's thinking, which served him well as a boy but does not serve him well as a man, has just validated itself.

Automatically triggered cognition also causes trouble in Harry's personal life. When a woman Harry cares about is quiet, he asks, "Are you mad?" If she says, "No, I'm not," Harry, refuses to believe her. He picks at her until she finally snaps, "*I'm not mad, I tell you.*" Then Harry says, "I knew it. You *are* mad. Why didn't you just say so in the beginning?" And at that moment, even mild-mannered women, those who rarely raise their voices above a whisper, start screaming, "LEAVE ME ALONE, YOU IDIOT." And Harry's disabling "silent-women-equals-mad-woman" conditioning is strengthened.

The experiences that result from our automatically activated thought system are real to us even though they have no reality to others or are not substantiated in fact. Harry, having no idea why women are provoked by his inquiries, thinks, "I'll never understand women. It must be hormonal." Harry has no idea he's caught in a thought-created cycle.

To protect ourselves from the adverse effects of automatically activated negative cognition, we must recognize when it has happened. The aftereffects are our clue. The aftereffects of automatic negative cognition are unusually disturbing feelings that result from an ordinary, everyday experience.

Insight arouses feelings of interest and wonder. Automatically activated negative thinking——fixed, repetitive and familiar—— arouses feelings of insecurity. When you walk into a hospital and your palms start to sweat, that isn't an insight that you have something real to fear from this place. It's an irrational fear-response triggered from your past associations with hospitals.

When Harry's irrational fear about silent women and anger is activated, he has no choice but to lose his peace of mind and feel like an insecure child when a woman is quiet. Lois, a woman who has learned to recognize when she's been blindsided by the past, does have a choice.

Isn't it a Nice Night, Dear?

Driving home with her husband after work, Lois was talking excitedly about something that happened at work that day. When she stopped, there was silence, then her husband said, "Isn't it a nice night, dear?" And in that moment, Lois felt as if she'd been slapped in the face. Suddenly unreasonably, irrationally angry, she had a strong urge to choke the man.

What happened? Automatically activated thought, of course. Lois has negative conditioning from childhood about men who don't listen, at least in the way she defines listening. This ancient pattern was so easily triggered and so suddenly overwhelming, that it wiped out Lois's mental health in an instant. One moment Lois was a calm, rational, emotionally mature person then, in the next moment, when her loved one said, "Isn't it a nice night, dear" she became a crazed woman consumed with thoughts of violence.

This wasn't the first time this happened. It was the first time Lois recognized what was happening and made a conscious choice not to follow through on her raging impulses. Emotional maturity doesn't mean you never have infantile impulses. Emotional maturity is having infantile impulses and refusing to act them out.

Lois was holding her irrational feelings in check, when her husband asked, "Is something wrong?" Is something wrong? What a dangerous question. Lois, overflowing with what was wrong, had paragraphs, books, libraries, museums of what was wrong and it was him in particular and men in general. But Lois knew if she got started she wouldn't stop and would end stirring up something so unpleasant that it could take weeks for the air to clear. She'd done it before.

She'd get upset, attack her husband——accuse him of not caring about her, of not listening when she talked——but he didn't understand. A strange expression would come over his face and he'd say, "What *are* you talking about?" And she'd say, "Don't play dumb with me, you know *exactly* what I'm talking about," and he'd get so frustrated, he once slammed a closet door on his thumb and had a bruise for weeks. She drove him to it.

But this time, realizing she was overreacting to past conditioning, Lois saved the day and her husband's body parts. In one heroic moment of self-control, Lois said, "I'm too upset to talk rationally right now. Let's talk later, when I feel better. This is the best I can do right now. If you press me I guarantee, you'll regret it." Fortunately, Lois's husband isn't conditioned, like Harry, to dig into silence, for if he had, his probing would have triggered an explosion he would have had to deal with for weeks.

As it was, they drove home in silence and Lois' husband made dinner while she soaked in the tub, healing invisible wounds. Automatically triggered negative thought hits like a hammer to your emotional thumb. Even when the hammering stops, the hurts last a while. Lois felt off balance the rest of the evening, but the next morning she woke up feeling fine, the upset completely gone. Telling the story at work, everyone identified with it and had a good laugh. Understanding how an event in the present can trigger negative thought from the past, enables us to circumvent unteachable moments.

AUTOMATICALLY UNTEACHABLE MOMENTS

Unrecognized automatic negative thought from the past not only creates personal *dis*ability, like it did for Amy, Misty and Tom in a previous chapter, it also creates interpersonal *dis*ability, making it difficult, if not impossible, to understand one another, to communicate effectively, heart-to-heart, rationally, with patience, clarity and affection.

Nobody Talks to Me Like That

An angry client, court-mandated to counseling for driving under the influence, comes to the session in a defiant state of mind. The counselor, who perceived her father to be overbearing and demanding, bristles at the client's anger and thinks, "Who does he think he is? Nobody talks to me like that. I'll show him whose boss." Her negative attitude not only creates unnecessary stress for herself, but makes it impossible for the client to drop his defenses and hear what she has to say. When the counseling is unsuccessful she thinks, "His mind was closed. He wasn't open to change. These people are resistant clients."

This Will Teach Her a Lesson

A youngster talks out in class. The teacher, who grew up in an environment where she felt belittled and put-down, reacts to the past. Her underthoughts are, "This is disrespect, ridicule, contempt. I've had it up to here with people who take advantage of me and I'm not taking it anymore." So this educator drops a nuclear bomb to quell a mosquito and when the wounded girl begins to cry, the teacher thinks, "She deserved it. This will teach her a lesson." And it does. It teaches the girl to think negatively, fearfully about teachers, authority figures, learning and school.

An Outraged Father

A youngster is awarded a scholarship to a prestigious Ivy League school in another part of the country and turns it down for a grant to the state university. Her father is outraged. But he isn't responding, as he thinks he is, to his daughter's needs and desires, but to his own. Years ago he turned down a scholarship to a renowned school and he's regretted it ever since. His upset is not from his daughter's choice in the present but from his perceived missed opportunity in the past. Not knowing this, he allows this upset to cloud his mind to the extent that he can't talk to his daughter without making her feel wrong and pushing her away.

BREAKING THE CYCLE OF NEGATIVE CONDITIONING

There are two steps to breaking the cycle of automatically activated negative cognition.

1. Recognize what's happening.
2. Put yourself on hold.

Recognize What's Happening

When automatically activated negative thought strikes, you feel as if the emotional rug has been pulled out from under you. One moment you are a patient, capable, clear-thinking, full-functioning human being and the next instant you are emotionally impaired, overwhelmed, disturbed. If you don't know what's happening, you only seem to have two recourses: (1) to feel victimized and withdraw——your emotional tail between your legs, or (2) to lash out in self-defense. When you know what's happening you have a third option. You can put yourself on hold until your mind clears and your common sense is back in place.

When people overreact and lose their mental health, self-esteem or well-being over ordinary, noncatastrophic events, it's a sign they are responding to negative conditioning from the past. Wisdom is blocked, the fund of useful information is obstructed and feelings are either paralyzed or running wild. Strong negative feelings are red flags, warnings: *Emotional impairment in progress. Psychological functioning depressed. Go on hold. Breathe deeply. Get a grip. Don't escalate. Don't make it worse. Too much is at stake. Open your mind. Let go of the past. Come into the present. Reevaluate. Take a new look. Use your common sense.*

Going On Hold

In the car driving with her husband, Lois didn't have a choice about her negative history being set off, that just happened, but once she recognized it, she did have a choice about what to do next. She could either go ahead and weave a destructive drama out of old thought-cloth, or she could quiet the old thought so as to see the present situation more clearly. Making the wisest decision possible under the circumstances, Lois put herself on hold. It was the most responsible, mature choice. Going on hold keeps the brushfire from burning down the forest.

After a good night's sleep, Lois saw the innocence in her husband's remark and her part in his inattention. She hadn't told him that what she was saying was important. She didn't ask if he was ready, willing and able to give her his full, undivided attention. She mindlessly recited the day's high points, caught up in her own thoughts, going on and on, expecting him to be there, caring, hanging on every word and then becoming angry when she didn't get her way. Her expectations were unreasonable. She wouldn't want him to do that to her.

If all thought was consciously called and directed, we could avoid most of the difficulty in life. However, this is not so. Every day we are at the effect of involuntary thought that ties us to the past. If Harry doesn't learn to recognize and sidestep his negative conditioning, his tombstone will read: "Here Lies Harry, Old Before His Time, Driven To The Grave By Quiet Women." Fortunately, automatic thought isn't all bad. It has many advantages.

ADVANTAGES OF AUTOMATICALLY ACTIVATED THOUGHT

Because of automatically activated stored thought, we don't have to relearn the language or the name of our dog every morning. Because of stored thought we drive to work without thinking about operating the car or navigating the route so our mind is free to watch the traffic, contemplate the sunrise or plan a math lesson. Because of stored thought we can type eighty words a minute, say the alphabet and remember our zip code without thinking about it. Automatically activated thought, a highly useful tool, only creates problems when it was dysfunctional in the first place, doesn't apply to the present, yet runs unrecognized and unchecked.

Positive Associations: Happy Learners

Although some distrust the idea of conditioning, it is a fact. We make unconscious negative mental associations and so do our students, clients and youngsters. Of course, habit and conditioning, by itself, is not bad. It's how it's used, and whether we are at the mercy of it that counts. Knowing conditioning depends on thought enables us to use it to advantage.

Informed thinkers know when they are responding adversely to negative mental associations from the past. They also make sure youngsters make constructive associations with learning, ones that help them fall in love with learning.

Learning is an activity of the heart. A student who gets good grades in math associates arithmetic with feelings of pleasure and success. A student who gets bad grades in the subject, associates it with feelings of dread and failure. A student who likes his English literature teacher, associates the subject with gratifying feelings. A student who thinks the biology teacher is a bore, associates the subject in particular and learning in general, with drudgery. When people feel safe, interested and engaged, they associate what they're learning with uplifting, empowering feelings. The more the pattern is repeated, the stronger the mental association becomes.

Kids learn best from people they like best. They learn easiest the subjects they most enjoy. *To predispose students to a love of learning, be as firm or strict as you want, use whatever techniques, methods or structures you want, but like and respect your students, love your subject and show it.* Then your students' associations with the subject matter in particular and learning in general, will be pleasant, constructive ones.

A parent who loves and respects his or her child is a natural teacher. Michelle is an ace auto mechanic, not because she was born with a special feeling for cars, but because she loved being with her dad and he loved fixing engines. John wins quilting blue-ribbons, not because he was born with a special aptitude for sewing, but because quilting was his grandmother's favorite activity and he, loving to spending time with her, picked up her enjoyment of it.

To create teachable moments, teachers make sure students, clients and youngsters associate learning with interest, pleasure, accomplishment, gratification and success.

These feelings open minds to learning and create a lifetime of teachable moments.

SUMMARY

There are two forms of thought:

1. consciously called and directed thinking, and
2. automatically triggered cognition.

To protect ourselves and others from the disabling influence of automatically activated negative cognition, we learn to:

- recognize when we are responding to negative conditioning from the past; and
- put ourselves on hold to wait for common sense to see a clear perspective of the present.

To create a love of learning, we teach so our students, clients and youngsters associate learning with the most uplifting, gratifying feelings possible.

Insight

10

The Heart of the Moment

The human mind is a magnificent force. When thought breaks open, even for a second, incredible power is released.

When I was five, my parents tried to teach me logically, step-by-step, how to tie my shoelaces. Eager to learn and make them proud of me, I tried to follow their directions but I couldn't get the laces to form a proper knot. Bribes, threats, rewards, punishments—nothing helped. Eventually, concluding I was educationally impaired, they admitted defeat. Mother, walking away, said, "Just be sure to marry a man who will tie your shoes." That sounded good to me.

A year later, getting dressed for school, I had my foot up on a chair, watching absent-mindedly as mother tied my laces, when suddenly, in a vivid flash of understanding, I *saw it*. In a moment of utter clarity, I *knew* how lace-tying was done, not step-by-step, first-do-this-then-do-that, but all at once from a place inside, a light came on and the whole thing was laid at my feet. Although I'd never done it before, in that instant I *knew* I could tie laces, in the dark, blindfolded, upside down or backwards. The failure of the past was obliterated, the present was bright with possibility and my options for a husband were considerably expanded.

No realization of Mozart or Einstein or Sandburg was more gratefully received, for in that brilliant moment, beyond learning how to tie laces, I learned how I learned: through insight.

This brilliant teachable moment wasn't simply a result of developmental readiness as described by stage theorists such as Piaget[1], Erikson[2], and Kohlberg[3]. I'd been developmentally able to tie laces long before I had the understanding to do it. This learning was not, as described in the learning theories from the work of B.F. Skinner[4], a result of associating a given stimulus with a wanted response. This learning didn't result from analytical, logical, step-by-step thinking, rote learning or memorization. This learning came by insight, a spontaneous intuitive, all-at-once realization. I believe this is how preschool children learn so much so easily. I believe they live in a world of thought open to insight.

WHAT IS INSIGHT?

Insight is a moment of realization, the good idea, the new thought or understanding that simply appears. Insight is that incomparably satisfying, "Aha!-I've-got-it," experience in which we *see* something all at once——just the way it is——in a way we've never seen it before.

Helen Keller, bereft of sight or hearing, describes an insight she had as a five-year-old. Miss Sullivan, Helen's teacher, gave her a doll and spelled "d-o-l-l," into her hand. Helen imitated the gesture although she had no idea what she was doing. Miss Sullivan tried to teach Helen that "m-u-g" is mug and "w-a-t-e-r" is water, but Helen didn't understand. She got so frustrated, she threw her doll on the floor and broke it to pieces.

Later, Helen and Miss Sullivan walked to the well-house where someone was drawing water from the pump. Helen describes what she later called "the moment of my soul's awakening."

> . . . my teacher placed my hand under the spout. As the cool stream gushed over one hand she spelled into the other the word "water," first slowly, then rapidly. I stood still, my whole attention fixed upon the motions of her fingers. Suddenly I felt a misty consciousness as of something forgotten——a thrill of returning thought; and somehow the mystery of language was revealed to me. I knew then that "w-a-t-e-r" meant the wonderful cool something that was flowing over my hand. That living word awakened my soul, gave it light, hope, joy, set it free! There were barriers still, it is true, but barriers that could in time be swept away.

I left the well-house eager to learn. Everything had a name, and each name gave birth to a new thought . . . every object I touched seemed to quiver with life. That was because I saw everything with the strange, new sight that had come to me . . . It would have been difficult to find a happier child than I was as I lay in my crib at the close of that eventful day and lived over the joys it brought me, and for the first time, longed for a new day to come.[5]

Insight can be dramatic, like this one, a laser-flash of understanding that explodes into thought packed with feeling and meaning. Other insights are subtle, muted, a new idea or understanding that slips into thought so quietly you don't notice it at first. Later we find a new thought has come in, a new awareness, a clearer view, a different perspective. The penny drops. *Click.* And there it is, the answer we wanted. Now we know how addition works. *Click.* We know how to do that tricky dance step. *Click.* We see just how to tell the kids about the birds and bees or exactly what to serve for dinner.

Nine Characteristic of Insight

1. Insight is a first-hand, memorable experience. Insight is an immediate experience, a sense of heightened awareness that is so packed with meaning you can't adequately put it into words. You can't explain why you cry at weddings except to say that you are momentarily filled by a feeling so touching, you are capable of no expression but tears. Or, walking down the street, thought breaks open for a split-second, and in that moment, you *know* you'll live forever. It doesn't make sense intellectually; it's not rational or logical. It isn't something you thought up. You couldn't convince anyone else that it's true. But it doesn't matter. Because of your experience you know it's a fact and that's all you can say.

Insight is memorable; it touches your heart and soul and leaves a lasting impression. Remember the first time you drove a car? Until then, you'd been a passenger, along for the ride, but once behind the wheel, you knew for the first time what driving was. You said, "So this is it!" It was thrilling. Insight is very different from memorization.

A counselor tells a client, "You are a worthwhile person." A client who memorizes the counselor's words and stops there will say, "I know I'm a worthwhile person but I still feel unworthy." This client has confused knowing with memorizing.

Knowing you are a worthwhile person is more than parroting correct words. Knowing is a deep, heart-felt understanding, an *in*sight. When something is interwoven into your understanding, you don't have to get up in the morning, look in the mirror and repeat, "I am a wife and a mother. I live in Philadelphia, drive a Buick and love my family." When you *know* something, it's so much a part of you, you don't have to think about it.

Memorizing truthful words can be the starting place for change if it reminds you to open your mind to new experience and wait for insight to bring it home. However, rote memorization that stays at the top of thought and never penetrates below the surface is of no value.

A student can memorize the dates of the Civil War, get an "A" on the test, and have no real understanding of the meaning of that monumental event. A person can recite the Ten Commandments perfectly, then leave the church and run ten cars off the road on the way home. If we're not conscious of what we're doing, memorization becomes pseudolearning. We think we know something but we don't.

Children can memorize information without internalizing its meaning. A child can memorize the rule, "Look both ways before crossing the street," recite it perfectly, then dash unthinkingly into the traffic. Wise parents set important rules in understanding by providing opportunites for hands-on experiences that spark insight. They take their children to the street and cross with them, not once but often——practicing firsthand, again and again, with real streets, real cars, and actual distractions——until stopping and looking both ways becomes an insightful, meaningful experience.

We don't play in the traffic, not because we've memorized a rule that says we shouldn't, but because we know what will happen if we do. We don't stay up all night watching television, not because we've memorized a rule that says we shouldn't. We don't do it because we know how we'll feel in the morning if we do. Once we know the meaning in a rule, when we've experienced the common sense of it through insight, we forget the rule and just obey it. There's an old Chinese proverb: *Tell me, I'll forget. Show me, I may remember. But involve me and I'll understand.* Insight, when it comes, is the deepest involvement of the mind.

2. Insight is spontaneous, effortless knowing that comes when forced thinking is quiet. Insight is not a mental exercise, something you control, plan or rehearse. Insight isn't something you do, it's something you allow to happen. Insight comes when vigorous thinking is stilled and thought is open, relaxed and spacious. When insight comes it brings effortless knowing——understanding, comprehension, recognition, creativity, enlightenment, clarity, common sense, imagination, revelation and originality.

3. Insight is intuition. "Insight," from the Latin, "to see within," is related to, but more enlarged than instinct in animals. Insight is not "superconsciousness" or "subconsciousness," but the ability to penetrate either. Insight is not an analytical thinking process, but a revelation from within that releases wisdom and creates genius.

4. Insight is relevant. Insights are relevant, an outgrowth of what we think about. Chemists have insights about chemistry; physicians have insights about medicine; educators have insights about instruction; counselors have insights about therapy; and parents have insights about child-rearing. If you're learning downhill skiing, your insights will pertain to moguls, and not broad-jumps. Insight is not haphazard but a perfect fit to our need.

Charlie, a sixth-grader learning to shoot free throws, had marginal success on the court until one day in practice, in a moment of insight he realized that the power of the throw originated, not in the arms, but in the legs! This simple breakthrough revolutionized his game and made Charlie a superstar at the free throw line. The teacher had carefully explained free-throw technology to the class and Charlie memorized the correct moves, but it didn't have real meaning until, in this moment of insight, Charlie experienced it firsthand for himself. That insight was the turning point that changed his game.

Through insight, Irene solved her seventh grader's poor attendance and tardiness problems. Every week Irene lectured her class about the importance of coming to school and getting there on time. She threatened and pleaded, but the problem continued. Then, one morning, Irene woke up with an idea so perfect she couldn't believe she hadn't thought of it before. That morning, and every morning after, Irene started the day with a surprise. She showed a movie, served treats, played a game, posed a puzzle, started a contest, anything she could think of to capture her students' attention and interest in an engaging way. Not only did the kids' attendance improve, they started coming to school early.

Through insight students solve the deep mystery of long division. After struggling, thinking they'll never get it, in a moment of clarity, the penny drops and they *see* it: the secret of long division is their's. It was there all along, but until it was revealed by *in*sight they couldn't see it. Now that they *know* it, long division is not only simple, it's fun. Geniuses don't make insight. Insights make geniuses.

5. Insight comes in a positive state of mind. People have insights when thought is open and relaxed. Mental struggle is to insight what a blood clot is to an artery. Insights only come when thought is free-flowing; that's why we most often get insights in the shower, playing golf, baking bread, asleep or just waking up, watching television, listening to music or taking walks. Insights come anytime, anywhere that thought is expanded; in forests, in traffic and sometimes, even, in classrooms.

6. Insight deepens understanding and ushers in a higher level of consciousness. Sometimes you look at a person and think, "I know this person." Or you read a passage in a book and think, "I understand this," and on one level you do. But if your mind is open, later, when you aren't thinking about it, new feelings bring fresh insights and your understanding deepens.

Insight is the dynamic inner process of discovery and rediscovery through which our truth, our certainty of today, becomes a stepping-stone to a higher truth tomorrow. Yesterday, we believed that learning involved drudgery and mental struggle. Today, understanding a higher principle, we realize that mental struggle is not a part of, but an impediment to the natural learning process. Yesterday we believed that people got too old to learn. Today we know that when minds are stimulated, the brain continues to grow throughout life that, despite age, we can enjoy a great zest for learning that keeps our minds ever-young.

7. Insight changes and expands our frame of reference. Insight expands our frame of reference by bringing in new information or showing new patterns in what we already know. We can require students to memorize random dots on a canvas, but we can't give them the insight to see how the dots form into a bigger picture. We can require students to memorize the letters of the alphabet but we can't give them the understanding of how those letters form into words, poems and philosophies. That understanding requires insight.

To teach the principle of addition, teachers introduce the concept of numbers. Not knowing what a number is or what it means, students memorize addition facts and hope these will be the ones the teacher asks for on the test. Later, through insight, their inner vision shifts and they advance from concept to understanding. Once students "see" what a number is, how it works and fits into the grand scheme of things, they are skillful mathematicians who can solve any addition problem, even one they haven't memorized.

Insight makes the complicated simple. Deeper insight makes the simple beautiful. Through insight we see how all the seemingly unrelated bits and pieces come together into a comprehensible whole. My lace-tying insight showed how all the twists, turns, strings and loops came together to form a simple, perfect knot. Beautiful!

Schoolchildren enjoy the picture of Isaac Newton sitting under a tree, getting hit on the head with an apple and discovering gravity. They also would enjoy knowing that it was through the experience of insight that Newton realized that the force acting on the apple is the same force that holds the moon in orbit, thus instantly enlarging and changing forever Newton's——and everyone else's——frame of reference.

8. Insight ushers in a higher level of thinking. Insight brings in a higher level of thinking. If, in a hot burst of feeling I think, "He's an egomaniac, an arrogant know-it-all who needs to be brought down a peg or two," that's not insight. That's automatically activated negative thinking out of my conditioned frame of reference. When I calm down, my feelings soften and I realize, "He's struggling with life the best he can with the options he sees at the moment." That's insight. See if you notice, in the following illustrations, a consistent difference in how people and problems are viewed with insightful versus conditioned thinking.

Lower-Level, Conditioned Thinking: "She's selfish, immature and irresponsible."

Higher-Level, Insightful Thinking: "She's struggling heroically with the only possibilities she sees at the moment."

Lower-Level, Conditioned Thinking: "He's pushed me away for the last time. I'm sick of the sarcasm, the filthy language, the contempt. He's hopeless. I'm wasting my time trying to reach him."

Higher-Level, Insightful Thinking: "He's like a wounded animal lashing out in self-defense. If I'd lived through what he's been through, I'd probably be doing just what he is doing. It's not personal. I can open my mind and be as patient as I can be, hoping for the best, and maybe one day he'll trust enough to let down his guard. If so, I will have an opportunity to change a life. If not, I will know I gave it my best shot."

Lower-Level, Conditioned Thinking: "This kid's got mush for brains. I might as well give up."
Higher-Level, Insightful Thinking: "He hasn't broken into the charts yet, but he's destined for the big time."

9. Insight comes with a pleasant feeling of surprise, relief or release. When we arrive at a solution with analytical, logical thinking, we feel the satisfaction of accomplishment. When we arrive at a solution through insight, we feel the thrill of surprise. It's that feeling of, Aha-so-that's-it! or I've-got-it-now. Or we wonder, "Where did that come from? That's good!"

Insight also brings feelings of relief or release. Sometimes you feel a click inside and you don't know what it means because it doesn't come with language, but you feel like you've taken a releasing breath that brings a sense of mental or emotional relaxation. Later the words for it will come, probably some morning when you wake up it will be there. It's insight.

When we are open to it, as we were as children, insight learning is a dynamic, ongoing process that expands and deepens our consciousness every day of our lives, altering for the better our way of seeing, knowing and being. Insight is among the most pleasurable and profound experiences a human being can have. Interestingly, the characteristics of insight parallel the characteristics of spiritual experiences presented in William James' book, *The Varieties of Religious Experience*[6].

- It defies description; it must be experienced firsthand to be understood.
- It brings a sense of certainty or profound understanding that is unreachable by intellectual means.
- It is of short duration.
- It carries a feeling of a superior presence or power.
- It is a deeply memorable experience leaving an undeniable sense of its importance.
- It changes the inner life of the person who experiences it.
- It changes the outer behavior of the person experiencing it.

An undeniable sense of the spiritual accompanies the scientific inquiry of human potential. Master teachers throughout the ages have known that learning, in its deepest sense, is a spiritual experience. True insight, originating from higher levels of consciousness:

- brings deepened feelings of affection, gratitude, compassion, optimism and hope;
- brings out the best in us and shows us how to bring out the best in others; and
- would never lead you to hurt yourself or another person.

WHO HAS INSIGHTS?

We've thought that insight/creativity/genius/imagination/ingenuity/originality is something only a few fortunate people enjoy because of a lucky break in the gene pool, and that the rest of us have to settle for less or do without. This is not true.

Insight is not serendipitous and rare, a phenomenon apart that belongs only to a few genetically endowed individuals. *Insight, an outgrowth of the thinking process, is the birthright of every thinking human being, whatever age, color, creed, education, IQ, experience or walk of life.* Without insight, I wouldn't be writing these words. Without insight, you wouldn't be reading them.

Through insight we learned to stand upright, walk, talk, read, write, compute and whistle. Through insight, people write sonnets, break world records, win Nobel prizes, crack jokes, raise moods and teach happy children to behave responsibly. All discoveries and inventions—wheels, light bulbs, polio vaccine, zippers, $E = MC^2$, hoola hoops, microwaves and Post-It notes—came from insights. Insight is the origin of the world's art and invention, the source of evolving ethical, humanistic and spiritual values.

INSIGHT: THE HEART OF THE TEACHABLE MOMENT

Insight is to learning what oxygen is to breathing. We can't directly teach the meaning of love, beauty, compassion or even the principle of addition for that matter, because principles are too profound and abstract to be articulated directly. Fortunately, while these things can't be articulated, they can be realized through the experience of insight. Helen Keller couldn't comprehend the words "d-o-l-l," and "m-u-g" spelled into her hand until the moment of insight, when she understood, not only the words but the principle of language behind the words!

This is what happens when people start out memorizing the alphabet and end up reading and comprehending what they read. Readers, whatever their IQs, have successfully penetrated the mystery, not just of words but the whole of language itself. Think of it! What great powers of comprehension we have when our mind is open to insight as it was when we learned to read.

Insight is a beautiful, spiritual experience, the way to higher levels of consciousness. Our most serious educational oversight has been to overlook or underestimate the power of the human mind for insight, instantaneous, profound understanding.

SUMMARY

Insight, that magical empowering experience whose touch leaves us changed forever, is a teacher's greatest tool and a learner's greatest treasure. Insight is the form of learning we thrived on as children with minds so open we were fascinated by everything.

Our greatest educational mistake is to underestimate the power of all human minds——regardless of age, sex, IQ, culture or experience——for effortless and profound understanding through insight.

Preparing the Mind

11

for Insight

*Ideas are like coffee grounds. They must lay quiet for a time
while the waters of wisdom percolate around them and create
the wanted brew.*

How do people learn? There is a growing body of evidence that
the power behind learning is the deeper innate intelligence called
wisdom, which is expressed through the experience of insight. Insight is an integral part of a child's early learning experience but
in school, when they learn to rely exclusively on logical, calculated
thinking, they forget their ability for effortless, all-at-once knowing.

When we rely solely on analytical thinking and overlook
insight, our thinking becomes one-sided, our lives feel out of
balance and teaching and learning lose their zest and inspiration.
To be and do our best, we must release the full resources of our
mind. This means rediscovering our capacity for insight.

Insight can't be forced, but it doesn't have to be rare or
accidental. To prepare minds for insight, teachers must know two
things about insight: (1) it comes from composed states of mind,
when forced thinking is stilled; and (2) it follows a period of input
and incubation.

To prepare minds for insightful learning:

1. Create the mood of learning.
2. Provide a variety of interesting, relevant input.
3. Allow time for incubation.

STEP 1: CREATE THE MOOD OF LEARNING

The critical factor in learning is the relationship between teacher and student. Positive relationships invite learning; negative relationships inhibit it. We can't get so focused on the technology of teaching that we forget relationships. Yet teachers often put themselves under such tremendous stress that their relationships with students suffer. I asked a second grade teacher, "Do you create a nice feeling with your students before you begin to teach?" She said, "Are you kidding. If I had extra time, I'd go to the bathroom." Oriented to the clock, we've little time for connection, kindness, compassion, caring, or listening. We have no time to stretch, absorb, savor, to lollygag, wonder, dream or envision. These things take time and we don't have any.

Hurry looks productive but it isn't. When our world goes fast, our mind goes fast, not in an efficient way, but in a frenzied way. Faster, faster. More, more. After school there's tutoring, gymnastics, scouts, little league, ballet and karate; then grab a quick dinner and do two hours of homework. If you think that's bad, wait until second grade.

To revolutionize schooling, to form a new model of education, go into your classroom and close the door. Then, stop the world. Find the place inside where you feel at home. Settle in, get comfortable, invite in your guests and turn off the clock. If your guests have to leave at eleven fifty-three, set the timer so you don't have to think about it so you can be there——fully present—— available and ready for anything. This also applies to counselors and parents.

You may only have thirty minutes but if you slow down and take time for eye contact, for smiling, laughing, touching, trusting and kindness, time will stretch out and seem like more. Don't do it because it feels good. Do it because that's the way human beings learn and grow best.

People learn best when they feel calm and safe. They learn most from someone they feel good about, someone they respect, someone who is teaching something they have a feeling for, someone who cares for them as a person and takes the time to let them know it. If you love Miss Carpelli, studying for her class is easy. If you hate her, studying for her class is sheer torture.

Teachers *know* learning happens in a compassionate, loving relationship. Teachers know that each of us has a slow person inside that needs a little time. But they get drawn off their common sense by legislatures and school boards who demand more and more and can't figure out why students end up getting less and less.

When people lose their patience and caring, when they get stretched and stressed, they lose their well-being, their mental health, their greatest teaching resource. In a composed feeling, working with insight, teachers accomplish in five minutes what would otherwise take five hours.

When your attention is on teaching instead of racing the clock or calendar, you naturally slow down and do the common sense things that you don't dare take the time to do when you're in a panic. Teaching instead of hurrying, you:

- Get your listener's undivided attention
- Arouse interest; make the message meaningful
- Break the stress and strain cycle
- Help students feel up to the challenge
- Clearly define goals and give constructive feedback
- Insure success

Get Your Listener's Undivided Attention

Just because you are talking that doesn't mean somebody is listening. In a roomful of students, some will be hungry, some scared, some are being abused or neglected at home, some are worried or angry or confused. Before you can teach distracted people——and everyone's distracted——you have to get their attention.

Melinda couldn't get her third graders to settle down, so in the middle of a sentence, she fell to the floor, pretending to swoon. The room grew quiet. Marilyn sat up with a smile on her face and said, "Now, can we do spelling?" She had their undivided attention.

Teresa, a high school art teacher, was lecturing on perspective.

I was holding a painting to illustrate my points but I could feel the class slipping away. I asked them to listen but they weren't listening, so I looked at the picture and in a moment's inspiration I said, "Look at the way the light is shining on that lady's butt," and instantly every eye in the room was strained on the picture.

Teresa tells what she did another time the group was drifting away.

I knew most of the kids had stopped listening so I stopped talking and started looking around the room as if I'd lost something. The kids, curious, asked, 'What did you lose?' I said, 'Your attention. Do you have any idea where it is?' The class groaned but I knew they enjoyed the humor. Now whenever I stop talking and start looking around the room for something lost, someone says, 'I know. You lost our attention. Right?' and they are back on track. No hard feelings.

Miss Crystal, a counselor working with groups of emotionally disturbed children, had difficulty getting these all-over-the-place kids to settle down and listen. She solved the problem by joining them in a small circle, chairs together, knees touching. Then she said quietly, 'Let me see your eyes.' Then, slowly, eye-to-eye, Miss Crystal whispered about the 'quiet, listening feeling' and they all enjoyed how nice it was. Now, in a small circle, knees touching, talking softly, Miss Crystal makes her most important points.

Sometimes when we are frantic, trying to hurry, to get this or that done in a certain time, a child asks, "Miss Crystal, can we make a quiet circle please?"

A counselor in Tampa remembers how her mother got the family's attention.

When we kids did something wrong, mother usually didn't say anything at the time, but a day or two later, she'd call us to the kitchen for hot cocoa. We'd sit around the table dipping our toast into hot chocolate and talking pleasantly. After a while, Mother would say, "There's something important I want to talk about. Is this a good time?" And we, warm with cocoa, would say "Sure, why not?" Then she'd remind us that we'd agreed to feed Poochie but lately we'd been forgetting and we'd say, "Yeah, you're right. We've been forgetting to take care of the dog." And we'd make a plan to get the job done. Those times were so sweet, it didn't occur to me until years later that it was Mom's ingenious way of slowing down and connecting with us to get our undivided, cooperative attention.

When you have something important to say, slow down, make eye contact and say, "Please listen. This is important." If you don't take the time to deliver your important messages eyeball to eyeball, up close and personal, your listeners will only half-hear or not hear at all. On our way out with the garbage we yell something over our shoulder and then wonder why the kids didn't hear it. True communication stops the clock and penetrates the little grey cells.

To be sure your message is received, ask your listener to repeat what they heard. It's surprising. What you thought you said is hardly ever what people hear. Communication is tricky. To minimize conflict and misunderstanding, don't assume you have people's attention. Approach communication carefully, thoughtfully, respectfully by laying the proper groundwork and then double-checking, just to be sure.

At social gatherings, I had the habit of setting my drink down, forgetting where it was, then picking up someone else's by mistake. I did this several times in Patsy's home. The next time I was over, Patsy said, "Before I give you this drink, raise your right hand and repeat after me," 'I accept this drink on the condition that I know where it is at all times.'" I pledged and we had a good laugh. That night I knew exactly which glass was mine and it felt good. The incident was the source of good-humored bantering that night, and other nights to come. Patsy, a school principal, created a teachable moment by creating a nice feeling, capturing my attention, then putting her message across in a clear, good-humored way that preserved my dignity.

This was in contrast to my well-meaning father, who trying to help me with homework, went on and on into the long, dark night. Lost in his own world, he never knew when I stopped listening.

Arouse Interest; Make the Message Meaningful

After you establish a feeling of goodwill and have people's undivided attention, then make it in the listener's best interest to hear what you are about to say.

- This is so important I won't say it unless you're listening. Do I have your ears?
- What I'm about to say will definitely be on the test. Write it down in your notes, underline it, memorize it, write a song about it; remember it!
- When you understand what I'm about to say, it will make you a happier (richer, smarter, sexier) person.
- If you want a happy, smiling, cooperative, good-natured mother (teacher, counselor), give me five minutes of undivided attention.

Be honest, objective, and straightforward. Use your creativity and sense of humor to spark insights. Be playful. Some parents arouse interest by sticking wax-paper notes in tuna fish sandwiches, writing poems on bathroom mirrors or putting Post-It notes on the television screen. It's unexpected. Fun. It gets attention with a positive feeling and sets a cooperative attitude.

Mr. Lee got everyone's attention when he said, "If everyone follows these directions, exactly, to the letter, they'll be no homework tonight."

A teacher in Oregon told her spelling class, "When ten kids or more get 100% on the test, we'll have a popcorn party." Her kids loved spelling.

A parent told her teenager, "Clean your room to my ultra-picky specifications and you can have the car tonight." Interest aroused, the message received, the room was spotless in record time. Happy teen. Happy mom.

A father got immediate results on a sunny Saturday morning when after an insight, he announced, "A picnic when the house is clean!"

Make your important messages fun, interesting, spellbinding, worthwhile and people will listen. The key to insight is breaking the stress and strain cycle.

Break the Stress and Strain Cycle

Recent brain research makes it clear——*the brain shuts down under pressure*. Fear of failure, anxiety, strain, and boredom——stressful feelings of any kind——block creative intelligence. Self-doubt dries up resourcefulness. Insecurity shrivels thought, freezes the data bank, activates negative, limiting beliefs and keeps insight at bay.

Creative thinking is linked, not with stress, strain and insecurity, but with good humor, playful attitudes and feelings of safety. An impressive body of research, as well as an impressive amount of clinical observation indicates that anxiety, doubt and self-criticism cause a person to function well below his or her ability.[7] Research shows that freedom from anxiety and pressure enables people to do the most creative thinking.[8] Humor and creative thinking also are related.[9] Before being given a creativity test, 141 Israeli tenth-grade students listened to a recording of a comedian and had a good laugh before the test. All these students scored significantly higher than the control group that listened to a recording about math. Research clearly links positive states of mind with increased imagination, ingenuity, originality, humor, fantasy and metaphor. Enjoyment, interest, joy and delight open the mind and release insight and free the power to learn.

Do you see what this means? To be superior teachers and excellent learners we've got to lighten up! Mentally stressed thought is so overfull, so impacted and agitated, it's a wonder we have insights at all. It recalls those little green shoots that somehow manage to sprout through the concrete sidewalk. What would happen if we relaxed thought, opened our minds to insight and gave our ideas room to grow even more insights?

There's a big difference between working hard and grinding. Working hard is fun, thrilling, and satisfying. Grinding is not. Grinding cripples insight. When you try to think of a name that's right on the tip of your tongue, as long as you are straining to remember, you can't think of it. But when you think about something else, the name pops effortlessly into your mind.

Or, when you try to solve a problem and reach an impasse, the more you think about it, the more confused you get. Eventually, frustrated, you give up and go for a walk. Then, in the middle of the walk or later in the shower——or even the next morning when you wake up——there it is: insight. And there is the solution you've been looking for.

In positive states of mind, it's easy to pay attention and have insights. In negative states of mind we read the same paragraph five times and still don't know what it says. When we don't feel our best we don't feel up to the challenge.

Help Students Feel Up to the Challenge

People have insights when they feel up to the challenge. If your son is watching MTV instead of doing his homework, if you think, "I can handle this situation with creativity and good humor," that thought will start your good ideas rolling. If you feel overwhelmed and think "this is too much for me to handle," your thought will cloud over and keep the good ideas at bay.

When people feel there is too little demand on their ability, they are bored, unchallenged. When they feel there is too much demand, they feel bewildered, defeated. *Insight occurs in the space between boredom and anxiety.*

Define Goals Clearly and Give Constructive Feedback

People's minds are open to insight when they are given a clear understanding of what they're aiming for and the differences their actions make. If you're unclear where you're going or if you work in the dark with no feedback, it's difficult to work insightfully.

Insure Success

Success opens the mind to insight. Reassurance is always justified. One statement such as, "Well done," or "This is much better," or "I see you are really working hard," or "I know it's hard," is pure gold because it gives hope. Human beings thrive on hope. Without it, they give up. To kindle your students, client's or youngster's potential and make them hungry for more, let them succeed, then stand back and watch the insights come.

Cynthia, a special education teacher tells how she builds success into her teaching by simply telling the truth. Ramone, age eight, had been struggling to write his letters on the line. Finally, when he handed in his work, Cynthia said, "The letters are neat. I appreciate that. It can be hard to write on the line. It's a pleasure to see such genuine effort!" Ramone kissed his paper. "I am a good writer," he announced, "I want to do more."

Step one, to prepare minds for insightful learning, is to create the mood of learning. Step two is to provide a variety of input.

STEP TWO: PROVIDE A VARIETY OF INTERESTING, RELEVANT INPUT

To stimulate insight, provide a fascinating variety of ideas, information, stories, models, prototypes, opinions, examples and illustrations. Get students involved asking questions, practicing, experimenting, doing projects, observing, reflecting, dreaming, imagining—keeping their minds open to images and impressions of all kinds. Use different approaches, interesting materials and provide plenty of hands-on experience. Ask feedback questions, "How are we doing? Are you with me? Does that make sense? Am I making this clear? Can we move to the next point?" Learning is a contact sport.

Some people believe if they've said something once, that's enough. But the things we know well are things we've heard again and again. Master teachers, parents and counselors give input willingly, happily, patiently, remembering always that slow person we all have inside, the one that needs a little time.

A gardener plants good seeds in fertile ground and trusts them to grow. A teacher plants good input into attentive minds and waits for it to germinate into insight. In learning, the germination period, where concepts grow into understanding, is called incubation.

STEP THREE: PROVIDE TIME FOR INCUBATION

Incubation is called putting an idea, "on the back burner." It is the period in which the mind integrates ideas that we aren't consciously thinking about. Later, when the process is complete, we get the "percolated" idea back, it bubbles to conscious thought as insight.

A rest, a change of scenery, walking in the park, reading the paper, watching television, eating lunch, taking a nap——these periods when the mind integrates input——are important to insightful learning.

Many people, trying to learn something new, say, "I don't get it. I'll never understand." When I advise them to relax, think about something else and wait for understanding to dawn from within, they say, "I did that, but it's not working." This is like the insecure gardener who plants seeds, then every day digs them up to see how they are doing and says, "I don't get it. I planted these seeds, but they're not doing anything."

Presenters that start workshops at 7:30 in the morning and go nonstop until 8:30 at night don't accomplish as much as they think they do. Thinkers have saturation levels. When the cup is full, it's useless to keep pouring. When people's minds are full, they stop listening. We've all developed the ability to look attentive while we're thinking about something else.

Inspiration is primed with solitude, playfulness, and idleness. A feather floats down from the sky. You grab for it but the act of grabbing disturbs the air and the feather bobs beyond your reach. The harder you try to seize the feather, the farther away it goes, but if you stand under it quietly with your hand open, it falls right into it.

Preschool youngsters don't struggle with learning. They don't get bored. They go full speed ahead until their interest wanes then they stop and go on to something else. When something stops being fun, they set it aside and come back to it later when their mind is fresh. Learning this way is not plodding and difficult, it's a breath-taking free-fall into adventure.

When we force thinking, we run into something psychologists call functional fixity.

Functional Fixity

Functional fixity is forcing thought so hard there's no room for new impressions. Rita was frustrated because her car was dirty and her son wouldn't wash it. Suffering from "functional fixity" ——seeing only one way to get what she wanted——Rita hinted, begged and threatened. When this didn't work, she put the problem on the mental back burner. One morning driving to work, the fool-proof solution appeared: she could take the automobile through the car-wash when she filled up with gas! No nagging, coercion, resistance or resentment. It worked like a charm. To this day, Rita loves the car wash.

This solution was so long coming because Rita was fixed on the solution being something her son would do instead of being something she could do for herself. Turning the problem over to her deeper, creative intelligence, opened the way to a larger reason.

SUMMARY

The three steps of preparing the mind for insight are:

1. Create the mood of learning.
2. Provide a variety of interesting, relevant data.
3. Allow time for incubation.

Establish a positive relationship, get people's attention and provide plenty of input. When attention wanders, take a break. After a rest, minds will be refreshed, ready for more. Working this way is not an excuse for sloughing off or for a lackadaisical attitude. It is a responsible, scientific, research-based approach to learning.

When you stop pushing and slow down, taking time for incubation, to let your ideas and imagination percolate, when you take the time, not just to think, but to feel, connect and enjoy, insight is inevitable and learning is pure pleasure.

12

Facts About Moods

That Can Change Your Life

A positive state of mind is a person's greatest psychological power. A negative state of mind is a person's greatest liability.

Your teenager borrows your car, promising to return it in mint condition. Next morning, getting in the car on your way to work, you find the floor mats covered with sand, wet bathing suits on the fabric upholstery and the smell of decaying starfish wafting from the glove box. What do you do? Do you take a deep breath, count to ten and proceed with the calm clarity of a Zen Master, your behavior teaching a mature way to deal with unmet expectations; a way your youngster would do well to emulate? Or do you descend directly into madness, your behavior teaching ways best suited to back wards of mental institutions? Whether your response teaches Advanced Mental Health 501 or Nervous Breakdown 101, depends on the state of your mind at the moment.

A STATE OF MIND IS A LEVEL OF PSYCHOLOGICAL FUNCTIONING

- In positive states of mind people feel their best, behave their best and bring out the best in others.
- In negative states of mind people feel their worst, behave their worst and bring out the worst in others.
- Teachable moments originate in positive states of mind.
- Unteachable moments originate in negative states of mind.

A parent in a *positive state of mind* creates a teachable moment by:

- responding from her highest levels of wisdom, affection and humor;
- teaching, through her behavior, mentally healthy, emotionally mature ways to behave when one doesn't get one's way; and
- bringing out the most cooperative, responsible behavior in the other person.

A parent in a *negative state of mind* creates an unteachable moment by:

- responding from her lowest levels of wisdom, affection and humor;
- teaching, through her behavior, mentally unhealthy, emotionally immature ways to behave when one doesn't get one's way; and
- bringing out the most defensive, uncooperative, irresponsible behavior in the other person.

Have you wondered why one moment your thinking is clear, you feel on top of the world, behave exemplary and people treat you well; then the next moment you're thinking in a sack, feeling edgy, behaving poorly and getting back nothing but opposition? These changes in thinking, feeling, behaving and responding are due to shifts in your own state of mind. Our state of mind——our mood——affects what we think, how we feel, how we behave and the response we elicit from others!

Before I knew this fact about moods, I thought shifts in thoughts, emotions, behaviors and responses were due to changes in the external situation. Sometimes I'd think my family was loving, brilliant, definitely superior, and I'd be grateful to know them; other times I'd think these same people were inept, selfish, definitely inferior, and I'd feel sorry for myself for having to put up with them. *What a shocker to realize that my perceptions were mood-induced and not, as I believed, situation-induced.*

In hindsight I could see it. One moment I bristled at my teenager's sarcasm but another moment I thought the same remark was humorous, even endearing. Moods, more than remarks, determined whether I responded with a smile or a snap. From one mood to another, thought content, humor, compassion and patience varied markedly. Sometimes these changes were striking; other times they were less pronounced, but still in evidence.

This realization was important, giving me a power, a response-ability over my experience that I'd never had before. Following are eight facts about moods that will change your life, enabling you to create the most teachable moments imaginable; to feel better, more on top of things, more in control of your life than ever before.

FACT 1. MOODS COME FROM INSIDE

Although it doesn't look like it, moods originate inside. Here's how it works.

Unknowingly, we produce a distressing thought that separates us from our strength, wisdom and ability. Naturally such thoughts produce distressing feelings. If we accept these feelings, give them a foothold and allow them to accumulate, they create a pervasive emotional atmosphere; a mood.

A negative state of mind, a bad mood, a poor attitude or sour disposition——we have many names for this sorry state of mental affairs——is the end-result of thinking in a self-destructive way without knowing what we are doing.

Your most important power is to know: *you are responsible for your moods.* Negative moods don't come from cloudy days, paperwork or stubborn kids with minds of their own. When our mood is right, we enjoy overcast days, busywork and freethinking youngsters. Stressful feelings are not inherent in people, places or things; they are outgrowths of our thinking, which takes on a positive or negative cast depending on the state of our mind at the moment. The world outside is a reflection of the mood inside.

FACT 2. THE WORLD OUTSIDE IS A REFLECTION OF THE MOOD INSIDE

A mood colors our experience. Looking through a blue mood, everything looks blue; looking through a black mood, everything looks black; only what we're seeing doesn't appear to be mood-coloration, it seems to be the only reality that exists. This, of course makes us feel worse. Walking down the street in a depressed mood, eyes downcast, unsmiling, exuding an I'm-not-approachable attitude, you think, "Everyone's so cold and unfriendly. It's disheartening."

Moods work the other way too. An overwhelmed teacher went away for the weekend and on Monday she said, "I went to the country and came back in such a good mood that my class changed completely." In a positive mood, everything looks better. In a negative mood everything looks worse. But, when things are bad we reassure ourselves by remembering: moods are constantly changing.

FACT 3. MOODS CHANGE CONSTANTLY

Moods change. The mind is in constant motion. Lying in bed, you worry about paying the orthodontist bill, the next minute you are transfixed by the moonlight shining in through the window, the next moment you remember to feed the bird. The mind makes incredible leaps. Every minute you change. It's very dynamic.

The *state* of the human mind changes constantly. It's never the same from one moment to the next, shifting often even during a single day. Fluctuations in state of mind are such an integral part of our experience we rarely notice them or take them into account. Yet, aware of them or not, moods are there, working in the background, coloring our experience.

Cora, a drug-abuse counselor, wakes up tired, thinking, "I'll never make it through the day," and this thought adds to her gloomy state of mind. But after a cup of coffee and a steaming shower, she thinks, "I might make it after all," and her mood lifts.

Driving to work, enjoying the sunrise, Cora's spirits rise even higher and she starts getting good, creative ideas for the family group later that day. Then, suddenly, Cora's car swerves sharply and when she realizes she's had a blowout, her mood goes as flat as her tire. When Cora finally gets to work, thirty-seven minutes late——with oil on her silk blouse, a broken heel and a hole in her stocking——she's in a horrible mood that makes everything look much worse than it really is. But of course Cora doesn't know that. She thinks she has an objective, completely unbiased, rational perception of things.

When Cora's first client complains that life is hard and unfair, Cora wholeheartedly agrees, but there's no comfort in it. She feels no compassion or empathy. She repeatedly checks her watch thinking, "How long until this person goes away and leaves me alone? Doesn't he know I've got problems of my own?" Cora would feel better if she knew:

- She's in a mood.
- Moods constantly change.
- When a mood changes, everything changes.

FACT 4. A CHANGE IN MOOD CHANGES EVERYTHING

A mood is powerful. When it changes, everything changes. Cora lunches with friends, their cheery conversation distracts her from her gloomy thoughts and her mood raises. After lunch, in a good mood, Cora looks forward to seeing her next client. When this disheartened client——who is stuck in a negative state of mind and thinks it's life——complains about her situation, Cora says, "If you think you've got it bad, let me tell you about my morning," and she tells her story, not like a tragedy, but like a situation comedy. Listening to Cora's story distracts the client from her negative thinking and she has a good laugh, the first one she's had in a long time. When the client's mood lifts, she feels better, more hopeful, more willing to listen and consider options. Cora, tapping into the effortless flow that comes in good moods, generates such an interesting discussion that time seems to melt away. They part, glad for the time spent together. The positive outcome of the session was a direct result of Cora's good mood, which the client picked up on. Moods are contagious.

FACT 5. MOODS ARE HIGHLY CONTAGIOUS

Research shows that moods spread silently, invisibly from one person to another. Starting with one person in a bad mood, a whole class, office or family can be affected with *Ugly Mood Syndrome* without knowing what happened. *And remember, what's being depressed in negative moods is psychological functioning, the ability to think, feel and behave constructively!* The following interaction illustrates how negative moods pass from one person to another.

Negative Mood-Passing Scenario

> **Student:** I'm confused.
> **Teacher** (in a negative mood): What do you expect? You never listen. How often have I told you. . . .
> **Student:** I hate this dumb class. I'm not doing any more of these stupid problems.
> **Teacher:** Go ahead and fail. See if I care. Only don't blame me.

Everyone listening to this unfortunate exchange feels diminished. Bad moods, like emotional viruses, passing from one person to another, contaminate entire social environments with mental malpractice.

A wise teacher, parent or counselor uses the contagious quality of moods to advantage, to set the most desirable emotional atmosphere. *Intentionally projecting and evoking positive moods is the heart of creating teachable moments*.

Next is an example of how a teacher's positive attitude infects a struggling student constructively.

Positive Mood-Passing Scenario

> **Student:** I'm confused.
> **Teacher** (in a positive mood): How can I help. I see you did a great job on the third problem. You may know more than you think. I definitely see signs of hope here.
> **Student:** Oh, really? Will you help me with this second one?
> **Teacher:** Sure. My pleasure.

Everyone listening to this exchange feels uplifted and encouraged. *A teacher's mood is the most significant psychological factor in the classroom.* It, more than any other factor, determines whether the tone of the class will be positive or negative, functional or dysfunctional, teachable or unteachable.

A teacher's positive mood not only increases her ability to function her best; it creates an emotional atmosphere that increases a student's ability to function their best. Enthusiastic, cooperative moods in teachers evoke similar moods in students. Optimistic, open-minded moods in counselors evoke similar moods in clients. Accepting, confident moods in parents evoke similar moods in youngsters, helping them think, feel, behave and achieve their best!

A teacher's negative mood not only decreases her ability to function effectively; it creates an emotional atmosphere that impairs a student's ability to function effectively. Sour, apathetic moods in teachers evoke similar moods in students. Antagonistic, hopeless moods in counselors evoke similar moods in clients. Critical or insecure moods in parents evoke similar moods in youngsters! It's very powerful!

Mood not only determines the level of performance, it either maximizes or minimizes the possibility for misunderstandings and interpersonal conflicts.

FACT 6. COMMUNICATING IN NEGATIVE MOODS LEADS TO MISUNDERSTANDINGS AND CONFLICTS

People in low moods are touchy, defensive and reactive; their thinking is impaired, their feelings are dysfunctional and their behavior is irrational. If you're in a bad mood trying to teach, you'll be lucky if you don't end up screaming. If you're in a bad mood trying to learn, you'll be fortunate if you don't end up throwing a book across the room.

Imagine what happens when teachers in bad moods try to teach students in bad moods, or when counselors in dumpy moods try to help clients in melancholy moods, or when irritated parents try to deal with cranky kids. You don't have to imagine. You know.

When two or more people in negative states of mind try to relate, misunderstandings, disagreements, disputes and arguments are sure to result. In negative moods, there are no feelings of compatibility, no meeting of the minds. When people feel peevish, morose, defensive, scared, argumentative, hungry, tired or sick, watch out. Low mood. The moment is *not* teachable.

An insistent coworker, approaching Edith in a bad mood said, "We have to talk and get to the bottom of this." Against Edith's better judgment——she knew her office-mate was in a bad mood and that in negative moods issues don't get resolved——she sat down with him and he proceeded to let her have it. She was insensitive, selfish, pushy, demanding and overbearing; she didn't care about him and she didn't listen; if she didn't change, he would have to quit his job and it would be her fault.

Edith listened to her coworker ventilate his bad mood, thoughts and feelings. Then she said, "I'm sorry I've done something that's hurt you. I certainly don't want you to quit your job." The coworker, with a disgusted sigh, said, "If you cared about me, if you knew me at all, you'd know that I didn't mean it when I said I'd quit this job. I need this job. What's the matter with you anyway?"

Trying to resolve problems with people in a low mood is no-win. In the best scenario, you walk away from these encounters feeling dazed, like you walked through the looking glass into the twilight zone. In the worst scenario is that your mood drops too, you go nose-to-nose and say, "Oh yeah, let me tell *you* about selfish and overbearing . . . ," and you walk away from each other with your self-esteem in shreds, your well-being out-the-door and violence on your mind.

Low moods not only steal mental health, self-esteem and well-being; they also steal time.

FACT 7. MOODS ALTER OUR SENSE OF TIME

In negative states of mind, we have either too much or too little time. As a teacher with no understanding of moods, I'd start thinking about the forty-seven life-and-death things I had to do before the bell rang, then I'd feel panicky and start racing the clock. I'd begin talking the instant the bell rang and wouldn't stop until the last bell rang six hours later. When students didn't pay attention, I talked faster, louder, force-feeding freeze-dried bits of information from my numb mind into their numb minds. At the end of the day I collapsed in hoarse exhaustion as the word-worn, brain-paralyzed students made their escape.

Fueled by thoughts of, "Too much to do, too little time," students with minds of their own, those thinkers who wanted now and then to make an observation that would take us off the course I had written in ink in my lesson plan book, were a nuisance. They got in my way. Later, learning about moods and intentionally spending more time in positive ones, I began, for the first time, to orient to the students instead of to the clock. It was a revolutionary idea.

When attention lagged, when our thoughts were too distracted to begin or too full to continue, we'd stop. Right in the middle of Important-Things-To-Be-Learned, we'd stop and rest our minds for a few minutes. Our favorite thing was visiting, getting to know each other. Students were hungry to know about me. How old was I? Did I have kids? What was my favorite food? Did I believe in ghosts? Was I afraid of dying? Did I believe in kissing on the first date? And I enjoyed finding out about them, what they loved to do, what made them laugh, what scared them, did they have a secret they'd never told anyone, what were their dreams, had they ever invented anything. They were zany, silly, wise, touching, wonderful and funny. Then, after a few minutes of pleasant chatting, we were refocused, ready to take up the "The Summer Solstice Ocean Currents of the Northern Half of the Southern Hemisphere," with renewed vigor. Making friends with time, we could stretch out, discover, savor, think and incubate, those processes so important to insight.

Sometimes I worried because my students were getting less actual instruction time than their peers. But at test time, these students' scores averaged higher than the norm. Although I found elevated test scores immensely gratifying, I was most pleased watching reluctant students turn into receptive learners.

Racing time, I felt remote and overtaxed. In a tense state of mind, I said more and communicated less. Relaxed, unafraid of the clock, I said less but communicated more, saying in a few clear sentences what had previously taken paragraphs. I discovered that students in positive states of mind were able to perceive complex levels of meaning with amazing ease.

FACT 8. LOW-MOOD THINKING STARTS A NEGATIVE FEEDBACK CYCLE THAT BECOMES A SELF-FULFILLING PROPHECY

Mrs. Smith, a teacher who unconsciously gravitates to low moods most of the time, sees a lad gazing out the window. She says, in a strident voice that pierces down several halls, "John, were you born an idiot or did you take dumb lessons? I said to get busy on spelling and that means you, mister. Get to work, and I mean now, or you'll be writing those spelling words one hundred times each after school."

Mrs. Smith's low-mood perceptions lead her to believe, "Kids are lazy. I have to watch them like a hawk every minute or they'll never get anything done." Thinking of students as opponents, Mrs. Smith is constantly suspicious, on-guard, ever-vigilant, expecting the worst and finding it. Her negative beliefs lead her to control with fear. Unaware that fear makes insight learning impossible, Mrs. Smith feels justified dealing out rude retorts and sarcastic put-downs.

Ironically, Mrs. Smith is the focus, not only of the students' fear, but of their hostility as well. Behind her back, the students misbehave and feel their irresponsible behavior is justified. They think, "The old bat deserves it." Mrs. Smith screams in frustration and her howls get results as long as she is looking, but she doesn't dare turn her back.

This unhappy teacher, counting the days until vacation, hoping she makes it until then, berates the class for treating others the way she treats them, never realizing that hostility reinforces the very thing it attacks. She works hard but her results are mediocre. People don't listen from the heart to teachers they don't respect.

John reacts to Mrs. Smith's biting words by feeling embarrassed and anxious, and these mind-numbing emotions adversely affect his work. When Mrs. Smith sees John's barely passable assignments, she thinks, "I knew it. The kid is lazy." This unhappy teacher has no idea that her low-mood thinking is creating a self-fulfilling prophecy. Figure 12-A shows this negative cycle.

Figure 12-A
The Negative Illwill Cycle

Mrs. Smith's Thought
"Kids are lazy."

Mrs. Smith's Reaction: Mrs Smith's Feeling:
"I knew it. Kids are lazy."   Suspicion, Vigilance

John's Behavior: Mrs. Smith's Behavior
Careless Work   Sarcasm, Put-Down

John's Feeling:
Self-Consciousness, Anxiety

Mrs. Smith, unknowingly caught in a negative feedback loop, finds daily proof to support her low-mood beliefs. She also finds teaching stressful and unrewarding, not because she lacks skill or desire, but because her negative state of mind undermines her abilities. Ironically, if Mrs. Smith allowed herself to soften and slip into a more positive state of mind, she'd realize John didn't mean any harm, that all she had to do was quietly ask him, without insult or innuendo, to take his seat. John, more than likely, would be happy to comply. Happy children love to please people they like and respect.

Fortunately, positive moods also create feedback cycles. Mrs. Jones, the teacher next door, relies on her positive state of mind to ease her wisely through the day, enabling her to draw out and nurture the best in herself and others. Mrs. Jones's positive mood enables her to see teaching, not as a struggle between opponents, but as a cooperative, team effort.

Mrs. Jones sets the highest standards of behavior and achievement, which she implements by guiding, rather than attacking; teaching, rather than insulting. She treats students the way she wants them to treat her, with kindness and respect, and they, in return, treat her with goodwill and do what they can to please her. Figure 12-B shows how this positive cycle works.

Figure 12-B
The Positive Goodwill Cycle

Mrs. Jones's Thought
"Kids love to excel."

Mrs. Jones's Reaction
"I knew it. Kids love to excel."

Mrs. Jones's Feeling
Confidence, Respect

John's Behavior
Good Work

Mrs. Jones's Behavior
Encouragement, Support

John's Feeling
Self-Confidence, Enthusiasm

This teacher loves her work and, through her eyes, children see themselves as capable, at home in the world, destined for greatness. Kids enjoy plotting against Mrs. Smith, but they love pleasing Mrs. Jones. It's all state of mind.

SUMMARY

A positive state of mind is an accelerated state of psychological functioning. A negative state of mind is an impaired level of functioning. There are eight facts about moods everyone should know:

1. Moods come from inside.
2. The world outside is a reflection of the world inside.
3. Moods change constantly.
4. A change in mood changes everything.
5. Moods are contagious.
6. Communicating in negative moods leads to misunderstandings and conflicts.
7. Moods alter our sense of time.
8. Low-mood thinking starts a negative feedback cycle that becomes a self-fulfilling prophecy.

In positive moods we are at our best and we bring out the best in others. In negative moods we are at our worst and bring out the worst in others. Happiness is more than just a pleasant feeling, it is the source of our mental health, insight, wisdom, self-esteem and well-being, the heart and soul of the successful learning process.

13 How Moods Affect Your Performance

Negative states of mind (bad moods) are the number one cause of poor achievement, low productivity, mediocrity and failure.

In positive states of mind people are at their peak of power. Their greatest potential emerges. Morale is high; attitude is pleasant. We feel balanced, confident, optimistic, and able to cope with whatever comes. In positive states of mind the personal qualities we value most——clarity, wisdom, compassion, patience, courage, flexibility and good humor——are right on the surface, ours for the taking. We don't have to conjure them up or work for them. In a good mood, they are already there. Positive states of mind (good moods) are the number one source of self-control, motivation, productivity, excellence and success. All this changes when our state of mind shifts.

In negative states of mind, feeling overstretched and underappreciated, everything seems more serious and difficult than it really is. Losing our clarity, objectivity and sense of humor, morale drops and interest sags. Performance drops. In negative states of mind, all our most unpleasant impulses——impatience, irritability, suspiciousness, intolerance, inflexibility——are right on the surface. Other people's habits, the ones we thought were cute, even endearing, when we were in a positive state of mind, grate like fingernails on a chalkboard when we are in a negative one.

In negative states of mind, we feel mired in bad habits, organizationally impaired and without options, not because there are none, but because our thoughts are too agitated to see them, to make the most of what we have. On the outside, we look confident, in control, but inside we are wavering, uncertain. In negative moods, the teeth may be smiling, but there is no joy in the heart.

This chapter explores the effect state of mind has on thinking, feeling, behavior, self-esteem, emotional maturity and total performance.

THE EFFECT OF STATES OF MIND ON THINKING

Thinking in Positive States of Mind

In good moods, thinking is quiet, clear, creative, supportive and solution-oriented. We don't have to force positive thinking; we don't have to look in the mirror and say, "Today is the first day of the rest of my life." We *know* it's the first day. We don't have to put on a happy face or generate happy thoughts. We are smiling. We already have happy thoughts. Positive mood thinking doesn't deny or negate problems but puts them into a larger, more realistic context, one rich in options and possibilities.

In positive states of mind, we enjoy the productive, insightful form of thinking we call "the flow." The term "flow," coined by researcher, Mihaly Csikszentmihalyi[1], is the distinctive state of mind where teaching and learning is so effortless and absorbing we lose track of time. In flow-thinking, you do your best without worrying about how you are doing or that you won't get it just right. In the flow state of mind, the right action arises by itself. John, a high school principal, relates this story about being in the flow state of mind:

> I had a complicated presentation to make to the staff but the minute I stepped to the podium, my mind cleared and words started coming on their own. Without referring to notes, I knew exactly what to say. After the talk, people couldn't stop complimenting me. It was fantastic.

Teaching and learning in this positive state of mind isn't drudgery, but like a game of volleyball at the beach. You feel challenged. You're working hard but you feel up to it. You're stretching your limits, expanding your capabilities. It's exhilarating. Evelyn, a math teacher in a private school describes this experience in the flow state:

> One day Ralph was sitting in the back row, *not* doing his assignment, as usual, when I went back and sat beside him. I had no idea what I was going to do but I was in a good mood so I knew I'd come up with something. Following an impulse, I said, "If you aren't going to do those problems, do you mind if I do them. I love doing math." Ralph gave me a quizzical look, shoved his paper over to me and watched as I began solving the problems.
>
> After I'd done several problems, Ralph said, "How did you do that? I don't get it." It was the first time Ralph had expressed any interest. I began showing him what I'd done and before I knew it, kids were gathered all around the desk, listening. Just like Tom Sawyer whitewashing the fence, the kids started begging for a turn at the problems. Ralph said, "Hey, get out of here. These are my problems. I get to do them." I couldn't believe it.

The flow state is a wonderful, naturally creative state of mind in which everything goes just right without any particular effort on your part. A Girl Scout leader described being in the flow state giving a talk to the parents of her troop:

> At first I was nervous, couldn't think of anything to say, then something changed and I felt carried along by a river with a strong current. Words were right there, as if they were thinking themselves. Later everyone remarked how much they enjoyed it, how organized it was!

The flow state is a natural by-product of being in positive states of mind. Unfortunately, when the state of mind turns negative, the flow becomes a trickle.

Thinking in Negative States of Mind

In negative states of mind, the brain is in the wrong gear for thinking. In depressed, angry or fearful moods, thinking becomes agitated, cumbersome, depressing, and problem-oriented. Attention, concentration, and recall declines. Aptitude dissolves. Potential drops. We vacillate, hesitate, and forget. It's impossible to make a decision and feel good about it. When pessimistic moods enter the scene, wisdom, reason, common sense and good judgment go out the door.

In negative moods, everything seems wrong. The tendency to produce self-destructive thought content in negative moods is so common, most of us do it without being aware of what we're doing. We get up in the morning, look in the mirror and think,

> *Oh, God. Look at those bags under my eyes. How will I get through the day? There's that terrible third period class, the curriculum meeting after school, then I've got to get to the store, the post office, the cleaners, take the kids to music lessons, fix dinner, pick up the kids, clean up and get to choir practice before 7:30. I can't do it. It's too much. Life's too hard.*

All this negative thinking before we've been awake ten minutes! Thankfully, after breakfast and a hot shower, our state of mind rises and once again we're thinking in ways that enable us to accomplish the impossible, just like we do every day.

But, in a bad mood, everything is wrong. The coffee is too hot, too cold, too weak or too strong for your taste and the cup is completely inappropriate to meet your needs. One minute it's the pencil sharpener, then it's the kids, the job, life. Low-mood thinking makes the simple complicated, the innocent guilty and the lovable contemptible. In negative moods, up looks like down, blue looks like red and nothing looks right.

In negative moods, we think the worst and believe it. In low-mood thinking, we take everything personally. Those people aren't just laughing; they're laughing at *me*. The catsup didn't just spill; it spilled on *me*. The principal didn't chose Tim to be Department Chairman; he didn't choose *me*. You know your state of mind is low when a pat on the back feels like a slap and a smile looks like a sneer.

Bad-mood people can't think of a reason to smile. Some people, not knowing about moods, stuck in a negative state for years, haven't laughed out loud in months. The way they think, it wouldn't make sense.

Negative states of mind activate our worst beliefs. A parent, maintaining an affirmative state of mind when their child has a problem thinks, "This is unfortunate, inconvenient, and unexpected, but we can handle it." This empowering attitude is conveyed to the child who is strengthened by it. A parent giving way to negative states of mind looks at the same situation and thinks, "This is a tragedy, a catastrophe. It's hopeless. We can't handle it. All is lost." And this self-destructive belief is communicated to the child who is weakened by it.

A counselor maintaining a positive attitude believes, "This client has the mental, emotional and spiritual resources to turn the corner at any moment." This strengthening belief, communicated to the client, gives courage. A counselor, giving in to depressing beliefs thinks, "This person is limited, incurable. The best I can do is help him accept and cope with permanent disability." This limiting belief, communicated to the client, takes away the possibility for change.

In a depressed state of mind a teacher thinks, "These kids can't think, they don't care and teaching them is a waste of time." In a positive frame of mind, a teacher's beliefs are more hopeful, "These kids are okay. If I keep my spirits up, they will do just fine." See Table 13-A for the correlation between positive states of mind (high mood) and negative states of mind (low moods) and beliefs.

Table 13-A
The Effect of States of Mind on Beliefs

Positive States of Mind	Negative States of Mind
I (he or she) can do that.	I (he or she) can't do that.
I'm loveable, capable.	I'm not loveable, capable.
Let's give it a try.	That will never work.
This is regrettable.	This is catastrophic.
I'll start again.	I give up.
Tomorrow's a new day.	It will always be this bad.
I can handle this.	I can't handle this.

In negative states of mind, we worry about everything. If the principal isn't doing evaluations, I'm afraid my effort isn't being documented. If she is doing evaluations, I'm afraid she'll discover some inadequacy. If the secretary doesn't invite me to his party, I feel left out; if he invites me, I dread having to go. If my students come from wealthy families I worry they will grow up spoiled and unrealistic. If they come from poor homes, I worry they will grow up neglected and disadvantaged.

Low mood is the worry-state-of-mind. Low-mood thinking creates reasons to worry and then justifies them. If one worry is solved, two more slip into its place. In negative states of mind, unhappy memories, "should's," "have-to's," "what if's," and "if only's" orbit like satellites.

In negative states of mind, logic becomes illogical. In negative states of mind, logic goes to it's lowest common denominator. In low states of mind, it seems logical to spank your baby for crying at night. In higher states of mind, logic points toward understanding, patience and tenderness. In one state of mind it seems reasonable to doubt yourself, to think, "I can't. I'm not good enough. Nobody cares. Why even try?" In a positive state of mind, a higher logic moves in and thinks, "Why not? I care. I'm not perfect, but I'm enough. I can do the best I can."

In negative states of mind, the illogical seems logical. Ann, a counselor in private practice, enrolled in a dance class to unwind after work. One evening, learning a new step, she tried so hard to get it perfect that she burst into tears. "Damn, I'll never get it right," she thought, throwing her towel to the floor and running toward the dressing room. Then, suddenly, Ann stopped short. She said:

> All at once it hit me. There I was bawling, feeling like a failure in a class I was taking for fun! In a bad mood it seemed logical to sacrifice my happiness because I couldn't do a dance step perfectly!

Low-mood logic would rather be right than happy. In low moods, it seems logical to think, "I have a right to feel hurt and angry and by damn, I'm going to do it and don't try to stop me. I *like* anger. I *like* feeling frustrated, so don't try to change my mind. I've got a right to my feelings."

In the logic of low mood, one criticism is more important than dozens of compliments, one poor grade is more significant than years of good ones, one word said in the heat of anger is more significant than hundreds of words said in love.

Low-mood thinking justifies inappropriate, immature and self-destructive behavior. In negative states of mind, thinking and believing the worst, it seems logical to whimper, whine, snivel, moan, gripe, nag, complain and feel *right* about it! In critical moods, feeling smug and superior, it makes sense to blame, rebuke, intimidate, expose, manipulate, or ridicule. In a low-mood, self-righteousness seems justified, stupid behavior looks smart and immaturity masquerades as honesty.

A kid's bad-mood thinking tells him everyone is against him, so he feels justified throwing his book across the room, stamping his feet and screaming, "*No*! I won't do it and you can't make me!" From the boy's impaired perspective, this immature behavior makes perfect sense. Later, when his mood lifts, and he's thinking differently, he'll feel sheepish, contrite and puzzled; wondering what made him behave so poorly. In composed states of mind, immature behavior no longer make sense.

An adult's bad-mood thinking tells her it's appropriate to say things like:

- "With a few more brains, you'd be a half-wit."
- "What's wrong with you? Don't you know anything? Don't you ever do anything right? You're hopeless. I give up."
- "I love you. You owe me."

Low-mood people have a name that justifies judging, blaming, recriminating, complaining, and guilt-tripping. They call it constructive criticism. They can attack you for what you've done, they can tear you to bits because it's, "for your own good."

In a low mood, innocent behavior looks manipulative. A parent's critical thinking tells her that her two-year-old is misbehaving just to drive her crazy. This thinking justifies the parent's ranting, raving and pointing out the child's personality defects. A teacher's bad-mood thinking tells him the principal is picking on him unfairly, so he feels obligated to put on airs and tell the administrator exactly where to put his latest request. Bad-mood thinking says, "Do it. Kick the alligator in the mouth. It will do you good."

Negative mood thinking brings out the worst in people. In negative moods, people are stiff, overcautious, controlled and controlling. They make an art out of superiority; a science out of pontification. In constricted states of mind, feeling dinky and straitlaced, preferences become all-important. "If I can't have the VCR every other Friday at 2:05, I don't want it at all." "If we don't eat Italian, I'm not going." If the student's name isn't written on the upper right side, (not the upper left), if the margin isn't one inch, (not one and one-half inches), if the paper isn't three-holed, (not two-holed), white (not pastel), bond, (not onionskin), it's not an oversight or an inconvenience, it's a holocaust. In a tight state of mind, there's no room for flexibility, creativity, or options. "Don't talk to me. My mind is made up." See Table 13-B for the correlation between a positive state of mind (high mood) and a negative state of mind (low mood) and thinking.

Table 13-B
The Effect of State of Mind on Thinking

Positive States of Mind	Negative States of Mind
Focused, Concentrated	Distracted, Confused
Flexible, Open, Inquiring	Rigid, Closed, Fixed
Bold, Original, Inclusive	Cautious, Habitual, Exclusive
Self-Affirming, Enabling	Self-Destructive, Disabling
Organized, Efficient	Disorganized, Inefficient
Inspired, Broadening	Ritualized, Narrowing
Positive Content & Beliefs	Negative Content & Beliefs
High Retention, Recall	Impaired Retention/Recall
Insightful, Flowing	Blocked, Tight, Obstructed
Higher Level Logic	Lower Level Logic

Low-Mood thinking makes mountains out of molehills. Negative states of mind impair judgment. Overreacting, we escalate misunderstandings into full-scale wars.

Mr. Phillips returned to class in a rotten mood after lunch and found orange peelings on his desk. He addressed the class, "I demand to know which of you social deviates perpetuated this outrage. Who left these disgusting parings on my desk? Anyone with minimal intelligence would know this is my work area, not a sanitary landfill." The class, stunned to a person, was silent. Mr. Phillips continued, "Whoever did this is not only a sniveling sneak, but a cursed coward. Since no one takes personal responsibility for this offense, everyone will do ten extra pages of homework tonight."

Mr. Phillip's bad mood infected the whole class and for the rest of the period everyone was edgy and distracted. If Mr. Phillips had been in a better mood, he would have handled the situation gracefully, by saying something like, "Oh, just for the record, I like oranges without peelings but I don't especially care for peelings without oranges." The culprit would have gotten the point and everyone would have had a moment of comic relief that set a constructive tone for the rest of the period.

A person in a positive frame of mind promotes discipline with dignity and firmness; without elbowing, badgering or insult; without character assassination. In seventh grade, we had a new substitute teacher. When she asked for our names, Harley stood up and announced solemnly, "My name is Albert Schweitzer." We dissolved in laughter, watching to see what she would do. Instead of taking it personally and being offended, this teacher waited good-naturedly for the laughter to subside then said, "Dr. Schweitzer was a great man. I understand why you want to emulate him." Janet asked, "What's that mean, to 'emulate'?" The teacher said, "It means to want to be like him. Who would you most like to emulate?" Suddenly interested, we were hers. Maintaining her affable state of mind, this teacher maintained control of the class and created a teachable moment.

A child tries to pass out papers and they fall to the floor. In a bad mood, a teacher says, "Can't you ever do anything right? We're waiting." In a good mood that same teacher says, "Are those papers giving you trouble? Let me help."

A child, crying, says, "You never pick me to feed the hamster." In a bad mood a teacher says, "You think you're the only kid in this class; that all I have to think about is who feeds the hamster? Grow up and sit down." In a good mood, the teacher says, "Is that why you're crying? I'm sorry I overlooked you. Let's put your name on the board for hamster-feeding tomorrow."

A person's behavior is a reflection of their state of mind. Table 13-C shows the correlation between positive and negative states of mind and behavior.

Table 13-C
Effect of States of Mind on Behavior

Positive States of Mind	Negative States of Mind
Is Cooperative, Helpful	Resists, Fights Back
Excellent Achievement	Mediocre Achievement
Supports, Assists	Demands, Insults, Abuses
Takes Responsibility	Blames, Makes Excuses
Disciplines, Guides	Badgers, Nags

Minimizes Conflict	Escalates Conflict
Listens	Closes Mind, Prejudges

THE EFFECT OF STATES OF MIND ON FEELINGS

We don't think in a vacuum. What we think produces feelings. In positive states of mind our thoughts are constructive and result in affirmative feelings. In negative states of mind our thoughts are unconstructive and produce dysfunctional feelings. See Table 13-D for the correlation between a positive state of mind (high mood) and a negative state of mind (low mood) and feelings.

Table 13-D
Effect of State of Mind on Feelings

Positive States of Mind	**Negative States of Mind**
Happy, Optimistic, Hopeful	Unhappy, Pessimistic, Serious
Encouraged, Inspired	Discouraged, Frustrated
Secure, Poised	Insecure, Vulnerable
Constructive, Healing	Destructive, Hurtful
Friendly, Helpful	Disagreeable, Rude
Patient, Kind, Considerate	Impatient, Intolerant
Affectionate, Compassionate	Suspicious, Judgmental
Contented	Discontented

In positive states of mind, we feel optimistic, invigorated, in-synch, not because it's Friday or because we won the lottery but because we're in a good mood. In negative states of mind, morale hits bottom, we feel down-in-the-dumps and out-of-synch; not because life is hard and we've got problems, but because we're in a state of mind that makes everything look worse than it is.

THE EFFECT OF STATE OF MIND ON SELF-ESTEEM

In positive states of mind we have the composed, stable, self-reliant feelings of self-esteem. In negative states of mind, self-esteem twists itself into ego. Ego is a coin with two sides. One side is inferiority, the other is superiority.

The inferior side of ego is insecurity. On the outside, we look confident, in control, but inside we are uncertain, plagued with self-doubt. Self-critical to a fault, no matter what we do, it's not enough. In an insecure state of mind a student, through sheer mental struggle, gets an "A" on a project, but the grade only brings a moment's relief, for she's already worrying about proving herself as a capable student on the next test. A counselor, fear at his back, helps clients, but every day he worries that he's not up to the job. A parent, plagued by insecurity says, "Don't run, you might fall," "Don't laugh, you look silly, "Don't play on the rocks, you might slip," "Put up a good front but be careful." A child with insecure parents learns: life is hazardous and you're not up to it.

The other side of ego is superiority. These people look confident but their attitude has an arrogant, brittle edge to it that broadcasts, "I'm better/smarter/richer/higher/more educated or competent than you are." These are the, "I am the boss and you'd better not forget it," folks. These people know, not only what's good and right for them, but what's good and right for the rest of the world, and they feel morally obligated to set things straight.

Self-Esteem and Belonging

In positive states of mind, we feel sure of our place and value. This sense of belonging, of being enough——not perfect but enough ——gives us the strength to handle whatever comes. Accepting ourselves as we are allows us to assess ourselves objectively and frees us to make needed changes in ourselves.

In a low mood, self-conscious and unsure of our place and value, we feel driven to prove our worth, to appear to be more than we think we are. We reach higher, struggling to do things perfectly, not because it's thrilling or immensely satisfying, but because we're scared not too. Motivated by image or obligation instead of joy, we get stressed striving for superiority. See Table 13-E for the correlation between a positive state of mind (high mood) and a negative state of mind (low mood) and ego.

Table 13-E
The Effect of State of Mind on Self-Esteem and Ego

Positive Mood/Self-Esteem	Negative Mood/Ego
Security, Well-Being	Insecurity, Fear
Self-Confidence, Poise	Conceit, Arrogance, Vanity
Assertiveness	Bully, Browbeater
Positive Self-Image	Negative Self-Image
Pleasurable Achievement	Proving Self-Worth
Happy for Success of Others	Envious, Selfish
Objective Self-Evaluation	Self-Condemnation or Denial
Builds Others Up	Tears Others Down

In negative states of mind, the lovely, self-assured, it's-enough-to-be-me feelings of self-esteem turn into the disturbing got-to-prove-myself feelings of ego.

STATE OF MIND AND EMOTIONAL MATURITY

Our state of mind determines our general level of emotional maturity at any given moment. See Table 13-F for the correlation between a positive state of mind (high mood) and a negative state of mind (low mood) and emotional maturity.

Table 13-F
The Effect of States of Mind on Emotional Maturity

Positive States of Mind	Negative States of Mind
Takes Personal Responsibility	Blames, Makes Excuses
Feels In Control Of Self	Feels Helpless, Victimized
Objectively Weighs Options	Impulsively Flies Off Handle
Assumes/Expects The Best	Assumes/Expects The Worst
Compassionate, Patient, Kind	Impatient, Abusive
Solution-Oriented	Problem-Oriented
Self-Esteem	Ego: Insecurity Or Arrogance
Independent, Self-Reliant	Dependent
Affirming Feelings	Dysfunctional Feelings

Responsible Behavior   Irresponsible Behavior
Clear Thinking   Confused Thinking

SUMMARY

State of mind affects performance. It affects our ability to teach and learn. In negative states of mind, our best is just beyond our reach. Our thoughts, feelings and behaviors are operating on their lowest frequency and we feel inadequate, defeated and stuck. No matter what we do, it doesn't seem like enough.

In negative states of mind:

- Thought content is muddled, fearful and problem-oriented.
- Feelings are discouraging and unsupportive.
- Behaviors are based on our worst beliefs, our lowest logic.

In positive states of mind our most constructive potential is right at our fingertips:

- Thought content is clear, efficient, and solution-oriented.
- Feelings are affirmative and supportive.
- Behaviors are based on our best beliefs; our highest logic.
- We enjoy natural feelings of self-esteem.
- Emotional maturity is high.

In positive states of mind——in touch with our proficiency and craftsmanship——mastery, successful accomplishment and joyful productivity is ours for the taking.

14

Reading

the Feeling

People are smarter when they feel cared about.

Startled by unexpected movement, I looked up to see Danny slumped against the wall inside my office door, head low, eyes downcast, staring vacantly at his untied sneakers. "Oh, no," I thought. "Not again. Not now." But there he was, stuck to the wall like paint and he wasn't going away.

Ten-year-old Danny, a frequent visitor to the school counseling office, was referred for fighting, hurting people, talking back, breaking rules and creating general mayhem. Danny tried to be good, I know he did, but he was driven, a feather in the windstorm of his own wild energy, his arms and legs whirling propellers that shoved, grabbed, tripped and kicked with a mind and of their own. You could track Danny's whereabouts in a room by the complaints, "Ouch." "Stop that." "Get away from me." "Teacher!"

On Ritalin for Attention Deficit Disorder, Danny was helped by the attention-focusing medication when he remembered to take it. When he forgot, as he did today, he was a tornado in tennis shoes; windows shook when he passed. Now, slumped against the wall, he was unnaturally quiet.

Looking at the defeated boy, my mood dropped too. From that state of mind, I had no techniques, no words of advice or encouragement; I felt like I'd said it all before, hundreds of times. Not expecting an answer I asked, "Danny, what in the world do you want?" Without hesitation, Danny looked at me and said, "I want shining eyes."

A big hole opened in front of me. "What do you mean?" I asked, already knowing the answer. Danny said, "I want shining eyes. I want someone, when they see me, to get eyes that are soft and wet and shiny, like they have light coming into them from behind. Shining eyes. That's what I want."

Danny's words hit like cannon balls. A rush of long-forgotten feeling welled up inside and I knew exactly what Danny wanted. I wanted it too. All of us, whether we know it or not, are looking for shining feelings. We call it happiness or joy or love or wisdom or self-esteem or mental health or well-being. No matter what we call it, it's a beautiful feeling and we're all looking for it.

I think we're looking for beautiful feelings because we had them once, when we felt most truly who we really are, and we won't feel whole again until we get them back. When we look for self-affirming, potential-releasing feelings outside ourselves, we get lost, because what we're looking for isn't outside. The feelings we're looking for, the ones that make us unusually strong, aren't outside. They're inside. We feel them in positive states of mind.

Since peak functioning is correlated with positive feelings and impaired functioning is correlated with negative feelings, feelings become an invaluable tool in the teaching process. Teachers who want to bring out the best in themselves and others use feelings as *signals*, immediate feedback indicators of the present level of psychological functioning.

Positive states of mind signal that teacher/student, counselor/client, parent/youngster functioning is high and the best potential for constructive response is operational. Negative states of mind signal that functioning is low and the potential for detrimental response is operational. The importance of learning to use feelings as signals of levels of functioning in the learning process cannot be overstated.

Feelings are an infallible signal that tell whether our present level of functioning is high or low.

Positive feelings signal peak power-levels of psychological functioning. Negative feelings signal impaired, powerless levels of psychological functioning.

FEELINGS: INDICATORS OF LEVELS OF FUNCTIONING

Teaching and learning are such complex activities that we need a signal, a sure way to know from moment to moment whether we are on-track or off. That signal is feelings. Feelings are the guide, the psychological Geiger counter that tells us——with unerring infallibility——whether what is happening right now is productive or counterproductive, whether what is happening now is most apt to result in success or failure. Teaching and learning readiness is revealed by feeling. Table 14-A shows the correlation between feelings and readiness.

Table 14-A
Correlation Between Feelings and Readiness

Positive Feeling	Negative Feeling
Mind Open, Thought Clear	Mind Closed, Thought Muddled
Positive Beliefs Operational	Negative Beliefs Operational
Patient, Tolerant	Impatient, Intolerant
Responsible Behavior	Excuses, Rationalizations

Positive Feelings: Points of Peak Learning Power

High-functioning, focused, efficient states of mind are characterized by positive feelings and the constructive behaviors that accompany them. See Table 14-B for feeling and behavioral signs that indicate that a person is ready, willing and able to teach or learn.

Table 14-B
Eight Signs That a Person is Ready
to Teach or Learn

Feeling Sign	Behavioral Sign
1. Interest, Curiosity	Alert, Attentive
2. Patience, Composure	Poise, Self-Control
3. Self-Confidence	Willing to Try
4. Respect, Positive Regard	Teamwork, Cooperation
5. Affection, Generosity	Friendliness, Sharing
6. Pleasure, Satisfaction	Clear Thinking, Focus
7. Good Humor, Cheerfulness	Smiling, Laughter
8. Security, Safety	Participation

Positive feelings and behaviors are psychological *green lights*. They signal: *The feeling is right. Mental functioning high. All clear. Proceed using common sense.* One sentence said in love or excitement ignites more insight than hundreds of sentences of bland information.

Negative Feelings: Impaired Functioning

Low-functioning, unfocused, inefficient states of mind are characterized by negative feelings and the unconstructive behaviors that accompany them. See Table 14-C for feeling and behavioral signs that warn of impaired psychological functioning, unreadiness to teach or learn.

Table 14-C
Six Signs That a Person is Not Ready
to Teach or Learn

Feeling Sign	Behavioral Sign
1. Anger, Resentment	Complaining, Arguing
2. Frustration, Impatience	Lashing Out, Crying
3. Agitation	Tuned-Out, Talking Back
4. Boredom, Indifference	Half-listening, Daydreaming

5. Insecurity, Stress   Unclear Thinking, Confusion
6. Depression   Giving Up, Nonparticipation

Negative feelings and behaviors are psychological *red lights*. They say: *The feeling is wrong. Stop. Mental functioning low. Common sense, uncommonly low. Reason, unreasonable. Intelligence, out to lunch. Proceed with extreme caution. This is not a teachable moment. Modify the mood, change the feeling before you proceed.*

A SCHOOL COUNSELOR LEARNS TO "READ" FEELINGS

Until I saw the correlation between feelings and ability to function, I forged ahead despite the feeling. As a counselor, I tried to reason with agitated people, to talk logically with depressed people and to solve problems with clients who couldn't think clearly. Of course this did not work. Upset, confused people, can't think straight. They believe the worse and see no options. As long as they stay in that state of mind, it's useless to try to convince them otherwise.

When I realized that feelings were synonymous with level of functioning, I started "reading" the feeling to see if I could begin counseling or whether I needed to take time to modify the mood —to put my energies into helping clients change the state of their minds. When I learned to "read" feelings, I started creating teachable moments.

Working with a client, the first thing I did was assess the present feeling. If a client was upset I knew it was impossible for he or she to listen to logic or think rationally. So, instead of trying to problem-solve, I did what I could to change the client's state of mind. To help people change moods, I became adept in the gentle art of distraction.

Changing Moods: The Gentle Art of Distraction

Many upset people believe that the only way to feel better is to talk about their problems. But, unless their state of mind changes, they can talk about their problems forever but nothing will change because they're stuck in a level of consciousness where all they can see is the problems with no way out. Stuck in a negative state of mind, the more people talk about problems, the worst they feel; the worse they feel, the more they obsess; the more they obsess, the more fixed they become in a state of mind that has no answers.

As a counselor, I'd been trained to listen, but now, understanding thought and moods, I realize that listening to long recitals of low-mood agony only perpetuated people's misery. It keeps people stuck in states of mind where options and possibilities don't exist. The listening I'd been trained to do contributed to, not alleviated, people's misery.

Unwilling to continue a practice that contributed to people's misery, I learned to listen, not so much to the *details* of a client's story, but more to the mood or *feeling* behind it to determine if a client was in a positive, open-to-learning state of mind or in a negative, closed-to-learning one. First I tried this state-dependent counseling approach on students.

Listening for the Feeling. Using this state of mind approach took diplomacy. I couldn't say to an angry, get-away-from-me-I-hate-you student, "Look I want to help, but talking about the problem while you're in a bad mood won't help; it will only make you feel worse. So, I want you to be quiet. Sit in the green beanbag chair and relax. Read a book, stack blocks, listen to the earphones, anything that will distract your thoughts so your mood will change. When your mood changes, you will feel better, your mind will be clear and then we can have a good talk."

Of course this was true, but people in bad moods take exception to reason. Tell an angry person he is in a bad mood, that he will feel differently when it passes, and he will object, "I am not in a bad mood, you stupid twit. Don't try to tell me what mood I'm in. You're the one in a bad mood. I want a lawyer."

To avoid mental tugs of war——"Oh, yes you are in a bad mood!" "Oh, no I am not!"——I simply directed bad-mood students to the beanbag chair and told them to stay there and amuse themselves until later when we would talk. Then I busied myself with paperwork. No talking. No explaining. No room for argument.

The oversized beanbag chair was in a comfortable corner, surrounded by irresistable distractors, books, puzzles, blocks and small toys, anything that would draw students' attention away from their problematic thinking so they could calm their heated thoughts and slip into a more rational state of mind.

Watching for a change in student mood, I looked for evidence of calm, composure, interest or pleasure. The change in feeling when it came——which usually only took five or ten minutes——was so evident, I couldn't miss it. To test my assessment, I'd ask, "How are you doing?" and if I got a positive response, I knew the student was ready for teaching. Then we talked. In this more rational state of mind, our talk was simple and usually productive. It produced the most desirable results. We always parted friends.

If the upset isn't too big, a student's mood can be changed through conversation; by redirecting his or her attention to a neutral-positive subject, like the weather, the lunch menu, television or the weekend. Any subject works if it distracts from the negative thinking that is holding the bad mood in place. If conversation didn't dislodge the closed, cranky mood, I'd go to Plan A——Changing-Moods-In-The-Beanbag-Chair——which always worked to calm agitated, overheated students and prepare their minds for rational thinking.

Children who were worried, abused or hurting needed a boost to a more positive state of mind too. This was accomplished by giving comfort, warmth, caring, assurance or a feeling of hope. Children are particularly responsive to comforting, hope-giving feelings, behaviors or words; ones that make them feel strong and able to cope, instead of weak, hopeless and helpless.

As a counselor, I found changing moods to create a readiness for learning was extremely effective. No matter the age, intelligence, sex or culture, when bad-mood kids turned into good-mood kids, they were insightful listeners and courageous, ingenious problem-solvers. One six year old who had lost control of himself in the classroom had this to say when his state of mind lifted:

> *I need five more minutes. Then if you will walk me back to the room I'd like you to stay with me while I tell the teacher I'm sorry. I want to apologize to the whole class, too. They were only trying to help. I don't know why I took it all wrong.*

Recognizing an opening, a teachable moment, I said,

> *You took things wrong because you were in a bad mood. In bad moods, people take things wrong. That's what a bad mood is. Then, when the bad mood changes into a good mood, like the one you are in right now, everything looks right again. Bad moods makes things wrong. Good moods brings back the feelings that show you how to make them right again.*

If students were curious and asked more about moods, I answered their questions. If they didn't ask for more, I let it go at that, knowing there would be future opportunities to teach about moods. Using feelings to tell me when mood modification was needed to make counseling successful worked so well with students, I decided to try it with adults.

SUE, A TEACHER WITH A PROBLEM

Sue, an experienced fifth grade teacher, dragged into my office at three-thirty one hot afternoon and asked, "Do you have a minute? I've got a problem." Sue's problem was Aaron, " . . . mouthy, disrespectful, won't do his work and all-over-the-place. I just don't think I can live through another day like this." Formerly, I would have tried to gather information, analyze the situation and attempt to solve the problem right then. But today I looked at this exhausted, unhappy teacher and thought, "Negative Feelings. Low mood."

Sue was a professional. When her state of mind was in the right place she dealt with kids like Aaron every day without giving it a thought. But now, this minute, she felt weak, helpless, without hope. Instead of trying to solve a problem with a teacher too distressed to think clearly, I invited Sue to sit in the beanbag chair and said, "I'm going to get coffee. While I'm gone, put up your feet, relax, rest your eyes or help yourself to the magazines until I get back." Then I went for coffee and took my time so Sue could soak up the peace and quiet.

When I returned Sue was reading *House Beautiful*, looking more relaxed, managing a small smile. Glad to see her mood on the rise, I pulled up the other beanbag chair and for the next few minutes I directed the conversation to kitchens, gardens, recipes and other pleasant distractions, so Sue's state of mind would continue to rise. After Sue was more relaxed, I said, "I don't know about you, but this time of day, my mind is mush. Why don't you forget Aaron for now, go home, have a pleasant evening with your family and first thing tomorrow morning, when both our minds are fresh, we'll plan a strategy for Mr. Aaron." Sue, already feeling better, agreed.

The next morning I went to Sue's classroom and found her preparing for the day. She said, "Guess what. I had a nice evening and a good night's sleep. Then, driving to work this morning I had a great idea. I know just how to help Aaron and I'm sure it will work. I don't need your help, but thanks anyway."

I saw this mood-induced transformation repeatedly in my work. It never failed. People in negative moods felt stuck; people in positive moods had the perspective and wisdom they needed to solve their problems! It was a breakthrough! Reading the feeling and helping people modify moods so they could access their own wisdom was the easiest work I'd ever done. People were really helped. It was immensely satisfying.

There was one catch, and it was a big one. Before I could help other people change their moods, I had to be in a good mood myself. To do this, I became an expert at "reading" my own feelings.

PHYSICIAN, HEAL THYSELF

People——even mentally healthy, emotionally mature, intelligent ones——have bad moods. Teachers, counselors and parents are not immune to low levels of consciousness. We are human beings too, as affected by the ups and downs as every other person. We get frustrated, scared and nervous. We feel lonely. We grieve. We bring our concerns to work just like everybody else. This is only natural. But in a negative mood, my thinking was as confused and befuddled as the people I was trying to help. In a positive state of mind, I had two things working for me: (1) the common sense and security to work simply and effectively, looking for the most teachable moments by reading moods, and (2) my composure, which had a calming, reassuring effect on others.

Before I sat with a client, conferred with a colleague, met a parent or attended an important meeting, I checked my emotional dipstick. If I was a quart low——worried, upset, restless or bored——I knew I was mentally and emotionally impaired. Usually, just the realization that my psychological functioning was impaired was enough to snap me out of it and change my train of thought to a more productive track. If it didn't work——if I couldn't shake the negative feeling——I proceeded with extreme caution, making no sudden moves or earthshaking decisions. It was a form of prevention. I might not win this battle, but I wouldn't lose the war.

Using feelings to assess levels of psychological functioning was invaluable to me as a counselor. Later, as a classroom teacher again, I "followed the feeling," as a directional guide to teaching reading skills. Although I knew it would be helpful, I was totally unprepared for the extraordinary results.

MIGEL: THE RELUCTANT LEARNER

Migel, a shy seventh grade boy reading at a second grade level, wouldn't read and he wouldn't even talk about it. From previous experience, I knew positive feeling was the secret to opening Migel's mind, but when I even mentioned the "R" word, his feeling turned to ice and his mind slammed shut. *Cold, colder, freezing,* the feeling warned. *Change directions, quick.*

I opened my desk drawer, took out a package of gumdrops and offered one to Migel. Cautiously, as if the candy were contaminated with some invisible substance that would force him to read against his will, he tried one. I had one too. Then we each had another. He began to thaw. *Warmer,* the feeling said. *You're on the right track.* After a few minutes comparing the merits of strawberry flavored gumdrops to lemon, I asked, "Migel, what are your favorite things to do?"

He gave me a what's-she-up-to-now look, then answered cautiously, "I'm a diver. I've been diving since I was a little kid. It's my favorite thing to do." Ah, *definitely warmer,* the feeling said. *Go with this.* So, gently, respectfully, I slipped through the door into Migel's world and asked him to show me around. Slowly at first, then eagerly, eyes shining, Migel told me wonderful, interesting, intelligent stores about his diving adventures. *Very warm,* the feeling said, *Very warm, indeed."*

One day Migel said, "I'd like to show you the pictures in my diving magazines." Diving magazines! *Wow! Definitely hot!* In that moment's insight, I knew the secret to getting Migel to read. I said, "Bring them to class. I'd love to learn about diving." Migel looked at me, just for a moment, as if I might actually be a real person.

Migel brought his magazines. As he showed me his favorite pictures, told his stories and shared his diving dreams, he opened like a flower bud. *Warm. Go with this. See where it leads.* One day Migel found a picture he didn't understand. He said, "What is this picture?" I said, "I don't know. Shall I read what's written under the picture?" Migel squirmed, cleared his throat, gulped and said, "Okay, what does it say?" There it was. An invitation to read. *Breakthrough. Proceed with caution.*

I read the caption under that picture, then another and another. Migel, filled with curiosity about diving, asked me to read more and more until my reading became a natural, pleasant part of our time together. Then one day when Migel asked me to read, I said, "Why not read it yourself? I'll help with the words you don't know." Migel looked as if I'd asked him to dive headfirst into a vat of slime, but he grabbed the desk in a two-handed death grip and plunged in. When he hesitated on a word, I supplied it. He stumbled through that first reading awkwardly, but somehow managed to understanding what he read. *Slightly cooler but holding. Stand by with gumdrops.* So it was, motivated by his love of diving, supported by his sweet tooth and encouraged by a teacher in a good mood, that Migel began reading.

Several weeks later I said, "Migel, it's test time." He stiffened. "I can't. Don't ask me," he begged. *Freezing. Bring in the heaters, fast.* I said, "Migel, relax, have some candy and for goodness sake, don't forget to breathe. Read the test like you read your magazines and just mark the answers that make the most sense to you. If you don't like your score, if you're disappointed in it, we'll throw it out and you can keep taking the test until you get the score you want to show your parents." Migel gave me that "she's-demented-and-I know-it look, but he began. The feeling said, *lukewarm, pray for the best.*

Next week when I saw Migel I said, "Migel, you'd better sit and fasten your seat belt. I have your test results and some very good news. It's so good, you aren't going to believe it." He sat slowly, bracing himself for the worst. I said, "When you started a few weeks ago, you, as a seventh grader, were barely reading at a second grade level. Now you are reading at a sixth grade level." He said, "What did you say?" I said, "You've mastered four years of reading in eight weeks."

Migel asked, "How can this be? I'm not a reader." I said, "Start thinking about yourself differently. You are a reader, a good one. When you are interested in what you're doing, you are a very fast learner. You may not think of yourself as a reader, but you have just proven you are one." After we went over the test, Migel said, "Can I call home? I can't wait to tell my folks." *Very warm. Very warm, indeed.*

FEELINGS: WHAT TO TRUST

Robert Frost said, "Something we were withholding made us weak. Until we found it was ourselves." We've been taught to trust our feelings. Now, understanding states of mind, we know *how* to trust them. Mental health and emotional maturity is not blind trust in one's feelings when those feelings are anger, fear and despair. Mental health and emotional maturity is trusting one's feelings to tell you the present operating condition of your mind.

A Note on Being Human

A negative feeling isn't wrong. Not at all. Everyone gets down. Everyone has times when they feel blah, discouraged, betrayed, alone, and hopeless. This is part of being human. We have the seed of everything in us. Negative feelings simply tell us that right now, for this moment, we are thinking in a way that is disconnecting us from the best in ourselves. We can trust negative feelings to tell us we are:

- seeing the situation in the worst possible light,
- seeing few if any constructive options, and
- believing our negative perception to be the only interpretation that exists.

Mental health doesn't mean you never have negative feelings or bad moods. Mental health is knowing what negative feelings are so you don't use them as an excuse to hurt yourself or someone else. Emotional maturity doesn't mean you never feel scared or despondent; it means you have the wisdom to recognize uncomfortable feelings are outgrowths of the way you are thinking right now.

My friend, six weeks after the birth of her daughter, dragged into work one morning exhausted to the bone and said, "The baby cried all night. At 4:30 this morning I stood aching, crying over her crib watching her wail and all I could think about was a teeny-tiny little baby hammer." This woman *thought* about abuse in her lowest moments but she recognized her unhappy feelings as a warning: *Don't trust what you're thinking right now.* She would never act it out. Mental health and emotional maturity is being able to recognize destructive thoughts and feelings as outgrowths of a pathetic state of mind, something that will pass, leaving you back in touch with the best in yourself.

When you feel sad, let yourself cry. Crying is a way to clean out the pain. It's healing. When you feel scared, find somebody to hold your hand until your courage returns. When you are angry, express it in a safe way, one that doesn't hurt, until you come out on the other side. When you feel like hurting yourself or another person, recognize these feelings as crucially important warnings: "You aren't thinking clearly. Do nothing! Pull down the sails and ride out the storm until calm weather comes again." Feelings are okay, even negative ones. It's what we do with them that can hurt.

At any given moment, an individual or a group, a class, an audience, a staff meeting, a committee or a family will have a certain collective state of mind. Each state of mind has a different correlation to the learning curve. Positive feelings have a high correlation; negative feelings have a low one.

Wise educators, counselors and parents use feelings as feedback meters, psychological Geiger counters, to access the present level of functioning of themselves and others. Human beings are responsive to feelings. Learning to be aware of feelings like we are aware of the weather, without judging if it is right or wrong, enables us to create the most teachable moments.

SUMMARY

The key to successful teaching and learning is reading the feeling. Teachers, counselors and parents have the skills to do their work, but they do not always have the feeling to accomplish what they know how to do. When the feeling is sour, it warns: *"Wait! Back off! Regroup! Find a better feeling."* In a more positive mood everything changes for the better all at once. Positive feelings invite people into warm, nourishing learning relationships; they release potential and free the mind to learn.

Feelings tell us what thought is doing. Positive feelings signal open, helpful, cooperative thinking. Negative feelings signal closed, hostile, oppositional thinking. To create teachable moments you must do two things:

- Assess your mood.
- Assess your listener's mood.

If your feeling is positive you are ready, willing and able to bring your best to the moment. If it is *not* positive, if you are agitated or upset, the first order of business is to modify your mood. Find a more functional feeling. Then——ready, willing and able——your teaching will shine.

Going For It

Creating Teachable Moments

15

Changing Moods

Psychological First Aid

Negative moods passing from one person to another, infecting one person then another, is the greatest hazard to successful teaching and learning.

A teenage client said: "I have strong moods. Sometimes I'm so miserable I think, 'Why not just kill myself and end it all. But then later, when the mood passes, I think, 'God, I have all these incredible things to live for and yesterday I couldn't stop crying.'"

Some days break your heart. But no matter how bad things look at the moment, we must remember: moods change and when moods change, everything looks better. To create teachable moments we become masters of mood change.

To be masters of mood change, we remember:

- Negative moods pass.
- When they do, everything looks better.
- We can change moods.

As a young mother surrounded by crying babies cutting their teeth on my knees and scribbling Crayola drawings on my white painted walls, in my lowest moments I dreamed of running away and taking my chapped shins to a sun-drenched, adults-only beach at some tropical hideaway. One such black and blue moment, there was a knock on my door. Harriet, my neighbor, with Sasha her two-year-old planted on her hip, wordlessly surveyed the scene——the wall-to-wall scrawls, the drool-drizzled knees, the tear-stained cheeks——and with eyes filled with compassion——said, "Just remember. This, too, shall pass."

Of course, in my miserable mood, I didn't believe her. All seemed lost. But she took me by the hand, led me into the kitchen and made a pot of tea. Twenty minutes later we sipped steaming camomile, watched our robust children at play and felt incredibly lucky.

It's amazing. You get up in the morning, exhausted. The kids are fighting, the dog is barking, the phone is ringing, the toast is burning and you're ready to give the children away, take Fido to the pound, unplug the phone and move to a monastery in Seattle. But later, after a cup of coffee and a hot shower, your mind shifts. The fog dissolves and you're grateful for your full life. This transformation is the result of a change in your state of mind.

Bad moods pass. Knowing this may save your life or the life of someone you love. Bad-mood thinking says, "You will feel this bad forever," but you won't. Negative moods pass and the instant they do, you feel better, although nothing in the situation——except your mood——has changed. When things look pessimistic, optimism is only a mood-shift away. When things look depressing, encouragement is only a mood-shift away. Mood-wise people don't wait for a bad mood to shift, they help it along.

WHY CHANGE MOODS?

Mood research confirms: moods affect performance. They affect personality. In distressed states of mind people are nervous, obsessed, stubborn, critical, angry, guilty, fearful, and bogged down. They complain, avoid, deny and procrastinate, torn between a longing to fulfill themselves and a compulsion to please, many are a perfect fit for what Betty Friedan[1] described as, "the problem that has no name," or for what author Melody Beattie[2] describes as "codependent personality."

But when these people are in positive states of mind their personality changes. They are unafraid, motivated, resourceful, and supportive. They can establish rapport, disarm opposition, melt resistance, elicit cooperation, motivate the unwilling and inspire the discouraged. They do things for others, not because they *have to* but because they *want to*, because it is satisfying, because it feels good.

Negative moods wreak havoc when they pass undetected from one person to another like virulent psychological viruses, turning the clear-thinking, responsible and emotionally mature into the pathetically confused. Fortunately, good moods, like helpful antibodies, also pass from one person to another, lifting spirits and freeing potential. Teachable moments occur when people synchronize in good moods. As Shakespeare said, "When the sea is calm, all the boats can float."

HOW WE LEARN TO GET STUCK IN A LOW MOOD

Connie, a happy six-year-old girl, slips into a bad mood and feels upset. Her parents, not knowing it's just a mood, get worried and try to find out the cause of the problem. They ask, "Are you upset because you don't like your teacher? Are you unhappy because we expect too much from you? Is someone picking on you?"

At first Connie tells the truth, "No, it's nothing. Just a feeling." But her well-meaning parents can't accept that answer, so they press on. "Are you jealous of your baby brother? Do you feel neglected because Mommy works?" Again, Connie tells the truth, "I don't know. I just don't feel good." But when she's bombarded with more questions, Connie, a bright girl who wants to please, eventually catches on and says, "I feel bad because no one likes me." Her parents look at each other and heave a joint sigh of relief.

So Connie learns to validate her low-mood feelings by connecting them to something outside herself. Eventually, she does it automatically, without thinking about it. Originally, all Connie had to contend with was a passing bad mood. Now she's stuck in a negative feeling with a *cause*, something external that must be changed before she can feel better. The word spreads: Connie has a problem getting people to like her. People suspect it's her personality.

Children, before they learn otherwise, move in and out of negative moods easily. One moment a child is happy and content, playing with his toys. The next moment, for no reason, he is cross and whining. Nothing pleases him. He throws his teddy bear across the room and slaps away a cookie. Then before long he is playing happily again, the upset completely forgotten.

Before children learn to make something out of low moods, to justify them, analyze them, deal with them, figure them out or "get to the bottom" of them, children slip in and out of negative moods with ease. When they feel awful, they feel awful, there's no doubt about it, but it passes. Children gravitate toward happiness the way flowers turn toward the sun. That's their wisdom and strength.

To slip through negative moods with ease, to regain the happy, empowering good-mood feelings we had as children, we must take an active role in changing moods. We must learn to administer psychological first aid.

- Recognize you're in a mood.
- Take responsibility for your feelings.
- Disengage and regroup.
- Look for the lighter side of life.

FOUR STEPS TO CHANGING MOODS

Step 1: Recognize You are in a Mood

Negative moods sneak in when you're not looking. They don't have the decency to announce themselves, "Beware! A sour mood has just moved in and taken control of your thinking. Watch your step. Proceed with caution."

Your thinking won't tell you when it's in the grips of low-mood. That's why we rely on feelings. Feelings never lie. When you feel dumpy, discouraged, frustrated, overwhelmed and underappreciated, these feelings warn: "Be advised: low mood in progress. Take precautions!" Martha, a second grade teacher has no idea that negative feelings are low-mood warnings. It's 11:45

and Martha says, "What's the matter with you kids? We've got twenty minutes left in the period, four more points to cover and all you want to do is fool around. If you don't settle down, and I mean now, I'll start taking names and calling parents."

Martha's in a bad mood. If she knew it she'd create a different feeling around the experience. She'd recognize the kid's resistance as a sign they need a break. She'd set aside her points, take a stretch and have a few minutes of casual conversation; then she could continue with the kid's renewed attention. If you don't know you are in a mood, you think it can't be different and you close your mind to creative alternatives.

Step 2: Take Responsibility for Your Feelings

Low-mood thinking points the finger of blame away from itself. Bad-mood thinking says, "I feel terrible and it's *her, his* or *their* fault." *He, she,* or *it* is to blame. Martha's thinking blames her agitation on the kids' restlessness. If she wasn't struggling with low mood herself, Martha would see the students' behavior objectively, knowing it meant they were ready for a break. Only in low mood would Martha bristle at her student's inattention and consider it a problem instead of a sign to do something different.

Blaming your distressing feelings on something outside yourself gives away your power. When you take full responsibility for your own happiness, for finding it, losing it and finding it again, you are in control. That's your power.

You are the only person on earth who can make you happy. You are the only person on earth who can make you unhappy. This is important. Write it on the chalkboard, stick it on the refrigerator door, needlepoint it on a pillow. When you feel bad, realize it's a mood and take responsibility for your feelings, knowing that "This, too, shall pass." Then go to the next step.

STEP 3: Disengage and Regroup.

Low-mood thinking is compelling, seductive and fascinating. It thrives on attention. If you pay attention to low-mood thinking, if you get interested in it, take it seriously, fear it, love it, hate it or resist it, it will suck you dry before you know what's happened. If you justify a negative feeling, if you say "I feel bad and it's more than a mood," you obligate yourself to feel unhappy. See Table 15-A for beliefs that support or justify negative moods.

Table 15-A
Beliefs That Support or Justify Negative Thinking

What I'm thinking now is the only reality that exists.
I have a right to feel bad. I can prove it.
It's Monday, I have no choice but to be in a bad mood.
This situation is serious, horrible, catastrophic.
I have to be stressed. I've got too much to do.
Unhappiness is more meaningful than happiness.
Happiness is a superficial, trite, shallow feeling.
If I don't dwell on things that make me miserable something horrible will happen.
Worry helps.
Concern equals caring.
I'll wait until tomorrow to be happy.

No matter how challenging your circumstances are, you will feel more hopeful, more creative and able to deal with them when your mood is positive. Cutting yourself off from the option of feeling good, even when things around you are bad, is cutting yourself off from your greatest source of strength and inspiration.

Don't trap yourself on an impaired level of consciousness. The minute you recognize a low-mood, strike, take a proactive stance. Disengage. Doubt it. Be suspicious of it. Disbelieve it. Distract yourself. Take your mind off it. Don't give low-mood thinking a second thought.

When you step in something on the sidewalk that the dog left behind and get it all over your shoe, you disengage and regroup. You don't waste time blaming the dog, analyzing what's on your shoe or thinking about how unfair life is. You don't call up a friend and complain about it or think about it the rest of the day.

No. You wipe your feet and go on your way. That's what you do with low moods.

Look away. Look out the window, walk down the hall, change the subject, get a drink of water, call a friend, take deep breaths, say a prayer, go to a movie, or make a bowl of popcorn. It doesn't matter what you do to change your mind. The tricky part of changing your mind is that you mustn't think about it.

Allison, a mother who recognizes she is in a low mood, thinks, "I'm in a cranky mood. I'll just sit here by the window until it changes. Okay, here I am disengaging from my miserable feelings. How long will this take? Do I feel better yet?" Allison means well but she's still engaged in her bad mood. Thinking about fixing a low mood is still thinking about it.

Allison is like Mike, who is trying not to think about hot fudge sundaes. Mike thinks, "I will *not* think about a hot fudge sundae. I will *not* let my mind be dominated by thoughts of ice cream and chocolate. I replace the thought of a sundae with the thought of an apple." Of course, it doesn't work. Mike's thoughts are overflowing with ice cream sundaes. To forget hot fudge sundaes, Mike must *really* forget them. To change moods, you must *really* forget them. You have to intentionally, firmly, honestly, sincerely block them out by putting your mind somewhere else.

Mike engages his block-out mechanism to tune out the sound of the television so he can read a book. He uses it to block out the noise of the party so he can concentrate on one conversation. If you doubt the human mind is equipped with a block-out device, ask your kids to take out the garbage.

The Power of Distraction. One day, having lunch in a restaurant with my husband, I noticed that the room had become crowded and noisy. Since I have a belief that I can't enjoy eating in a crowded noisy place, I thought, "Lunch is ruined." But knowing about moods, I rethought, "To enjoy this meal I have to forget my beliefs and put my mind on something else." So I started talking about my current pet project and, before I knew it, everything disappeared except the two of us. The restaurant was just as hectic as it was earlier but I didn't know it because I wasn't thinking about it. That's the power of distraction. It gives you a new reality.

Changing moods is as easy as falling asleep. But like falling asleep, changing moods is something you can only do when you're not thinking about it. When you were a kid did you ever try to stay awake long enough to watch yourself fall asleep? It never worked. The next morning you thought, "Darn it. I missed it again." That's because falling asleep, like changing moods only happens when you aren't thinking about it.

Looking away from bad moods doesn't mean you deny that problems exist. Not at all. It just means you wait for the mental mud to settle so your thought will clear and your highest wisdom will rise to the surface. Low mood is not a time to make gains, but to minimize losses, as illustrated in Table 15-B.

Table 15-B
How to Minimize Low-Mood Losses

Recognize negative-mood thinking.
Don't feed it with attention.
Distract yourself. Regroup. Think about something else.
Later, when your thinking clears, reevaluate the situation
    to see if there is more to be done.

STEP 4: Look for the Lighter Side of Life

Open yourself to positive moods. Look for pleasant feelings. If you don't do it for yourself, do it for your children, your family, your students or clients. Do it to be resourceful, creative, in control, on top of things, to be an excellent teacher or learner. Don't rediscover the lighter side of life just because it feels good, do it because it's the most intelligent, rational, responsible thing you can do. And as Abraham Lincoln said, "Most folks are about as happy as they make up their minds to be."

It takes very little to induce a positive mood, *if* you want it. Everybody would love to be happy, but not at the expense of what they think. That's the catch. You have to want to be happy more than you want to hold onto your distressing thoughts. It sounds easy and it is, but the next time your healthy functioning takes a nosedive, notice how low-mood thinking tells you *most convincingly* why you can't possibly look away. Once you recognize low-mood thinking as mental pollution, then it's easy to look away.

To become master of the mood change:

- Find a reason to smile, play, laugh and have fun every day.
- Cultivate simple, small, quiet satisfying moments.
- Get plenty of rest, good food, exercise, fresh air.
- Create a friendly, cheerful, can-do spirit.
- Practice gratitude, peace of mind, humor.
- Do things you love. Listen to music, read a good book, take a bubble bath, walk in the woods, light a candle, or learn to fox-trot. Buy yourself flowers.
- Use thought to thrill yourself, to inspire and make you strong. Put the power of thought behind your dreams.
- Be easily cheered. Let simple things make you happy.
- Enjoy everyday surprises.
- Reflect on your good fortune. Don't wait until you lose your treasures to be grateful for them.
- Get your mind off yourself. Every day, do something for someone else without them knowing it.
- Take minivacations in your mind. Put your feet up. Breathe deep. Imagine yourself on the beach in Hawaii.
- Treat other people the way you'd like to be treated.
- Develop patience. No one is perfect. Ease up a bit.
- Banish the worry-thought habit.
- Ignore insecurity. It's only a thought.
- Communicate. When your thought is clear, let people know what's on your mind.
- Ask for help when you need it, a shoulder to cry on, a hug, a smile, or help with the laundry.
- Enjoy a good cry now and then. It cleans, softens your heart, makes you compassionate.

- Remember: when you lose good mood, it's not lost, just hiding somewhere nearby.

HOW CAN I BE IN A GOOD MOOD WITH ALL THE SUFFERING IN THE WORLD?

Perhaps you're wondering, "Isn't it irresponsible to be in a positive state of mind when there are so many problems in the world?" Millions of children go to bed hungry every night. We have the nuclear capability to blow ourselves to bits. We suffer from delinquency, drug-abuse, corruption, dishonesty and violence of every kind. This is true.

And the sky is blue. And roses grow on the garden wall and the birds sing love songs at twilight. Every day the sun rises and every day new babies are born. Every day sincere, caring people go to work to make our world a better place. Life is incredibly horrible and unspeakably sweet, depending on how you look at it.

A human being, like a radio with hundreds of stations, can tune into an infinite variety of things and whatever we tune in to becomes part of us. If we tune in sadness, we feel sorrowful. If we tune in anger, we feel enraged. If we tune in beauty, we feel inspired. If we tune in quiet, we feel calm. Whatever we tune in to, we amplify and broadcast to the world around us. We can't help but broadcast what we see.

When love and peace come in to this world, they will come through the consciousness of ordinary people who find a reason to love and see beauty in life. These people will change the world one person at a time.

What would happen if people took responsibility for their moods and didn't blame their unhappiness on others? What would happen in the world, in classrooms, offices and homes, if everyone gave up negative thinking, just for the pleasure of being happy and contributing their best? Perhaps, knowing now what we know about wisdom, thought and moods, we will find out.

SUMMARY

Human beings function more effectively in positive moods. The four steps of psychological first aid are:

1. Recognize it's a mood.
2. Accept responsibility for your feelings.
3. Disengage and regroup.
4. Look for the lighter side of life.

To create high-shine teachable moments, we have a love affair, not with disability but ability; not with criticism but with encouragement; not with what isn't working, but with what is working. To revitalize the joyful, impassioned energy in ourselves and others, we open to beautiful feelings, let them fill us and spill over to help others.

The Turning Point

16

Unteachable to Teachable

If you are adept at synchronizing yourself and others in positive moods, your teaching effectiveness will be accelerated.

Mr. Mann is exhausted. His hair hurts. His head throbs. He can't think straight. He was up half the night making out report cards; his son came to breakfast with green hair and an earring in his nose; the orange juice tipped over in his lap and the puppy peed in his shoes. The last thing Mr. Mann wants to do is face the thirty-five Crayola-chomping first graders that just exploded through the door. But here they are, all over him like ants on road kill. The feeling is clear: this moment is *not* teachable. What does he do?

Does Mr. Mann force business as usual, navigating perilously through the obstacle course of slimy noses, wet, hacking coughs right in his face, the arguments, the interruptions, the I-can't-do-it, it's-too-hard's, the back-talk, the tattling, "Teacher, Johnny just dumped his underwear in the turtle tank," the grim pronouncements, "The snake is gone;" or the dreaded, "I'm going to be sick," moving dangerously closer to *Teacher Dearest* with every step? Does this low-mood teacher forge ahead, teaching Weak Thought 101, Grouchy Words 203 and Advanced Unkind Ways 512, or does he pull down his sails, take cover, wait for the storm to pass?

It's ironic. In this agitated state of mind, when Mr. Mann needs clear, rational thinking the most, he has it the least. His thinking does not say, "You're in a bad mood. Ease off. Start slow. Give your attitude time to change, give your sanity, your patience and sense of humor a chance to kick in. It's the sensible thing to do. You'll make gains later, but this is no-win."

No, Mr. Mann's low-mood thinking makes it seem all-imperative that he forge ahead. The teacher next-door comes in to borrow a book, sees Mr. Mann's fragile grasp on sanity and whispers, "For God's sake man, show a film and pull yourself together." Excellent advice, but Mr. Mann doesn't take it. He snaps, "Honey, I'd love to but I don't have that kind of time!" She walks out shaking her head, knowing she can't argue with that logic.

Mr. Mann's low-mood thinking misses the deeper logic, the one that says, "This is not a teachable moment. Go slow. Get a grip. Get a cup of coffee, an aspirin. Pull yourself together. It's not a luxury, it's a necessity. There's too much at stake; you can't afford *not* to do it."

To create a turning point, to change an unteachable moment to teachable, Mr. Mann would have to:

- Recognize he's in an impaired state of mind, not thinking clearly or handling things well
- Override his burning desire to forge ahead at any cost
- Disengage and regroup; find a more stable state of mind

If Mr. Mann were mood-wise, he would institute Bad Mood Emergency Plan #5, in which Tim, who lives to recite, reads a story aloud to the class, giving Mr. Mann time to grab two Excedrin and a cup of strong coffee. After the story, Mr. Mann would gather the group on the carpet, pull out his contingency stash of oatmeal cookies, pass them around and ask, "What would you do if you were Boss Of The World For One Day?"

This impromptu language arts activity wasn't on Mr. Mann's list of Important Things To Do Today, but neither was his miserable mood. After the story, the cookies and conversation, Mr. Mann is in a more functional, congenial state of mind, prepared to face *Dick and Jane* awake, open, unafraid.

Miss Gomez, a teacher of severely emotionally disturbed adolescents, turned her work around by paying attention to moods.

When I'm ready to scream, I put the kids to work on something they can do without my help, and I sit at my desk and pull my sanity back together. I do paperwork or just look out the window. After I catch my breath, I can continue with patience and a sense of humor. I used to scream at the kids and kept them agitated all the time, now I rarely do. The kids know I take time-out for mood-change. When I'm on the verge, one of them says, "Miss Gomez, don't you want to take time-out," and I get the message.

The kids have gotten mood-wise too. One day a new girl came to class and all she would do was sit under her desk with her coat over her head. I tried to get her to come out but she wouldn't. Then one of the kids said, "Don't worry, Miss Gomez, she's just in a bad mood. When she feels safe she'll come out." And that's exactly what happened.

I asked Miss Gomez, "What would happen if the principal came in when you were sitting at your desk. Would she be upset?" Miss Gomez replied,

The principal would rather have me take time-out than lose control with the kids. She doesn't hear my screams down the halls anymore and she's noticed the change for the better in my work. She knows about my time-outs and she supports them.

I asked Miss Gomez how she handled her kids spiking emotional ups and downs. She said,

I used to teach no matter what. I didn't care if I'd lost my sanity. I didn't care if the kids had lost theirs. I'd press on, interrupted every other sentence by some distracting, irritating behavior. I hated it. No wonder I screeched. I didn't see any other alternative.

Now that I pay attention to moods, everything is different. I start every period with small talk to settle the kids down and get their attention. Before I start to teach, I sit on one of the front desks and we talk about something interesting. I know things about these kids I never knew before and they know things about me. Talking this way, listening to one another, makes us close, on the same side, connected, like family. We respect each other. These kids would do anything for me and vice versa.

When the feeling is right, when we're settled down, I say, "Well, we have thirty-five minutes left in the period. What do you say we do some math?" And they say, "Sure, why not?" I say, "You'll have to listen carefully because we've only got half the period left." And they say, "No problem." It never fails. I teach, and they are right there with me, really listening. Not fighting for attention, I talk less and say more. If the kids get off track, just a word or two brings them back. When the feeling is right, we accomplish in a few minutes what used to take days.

Miss Gomez documented three significant results in her work with moods:

1. Her student's achievement scores skyrocketed. Most gained four to six years growth in reading and math in a few months.
2. Their behavior improved dramatically.
3. They became intelligent mood-managers themselves.

The first year Miss Gomez synchronized teaching to positive moods, her students' across-the-board improvement was so substantial that by the end of the year most of these severely emotionally disturbed students were stable enough to transition back into regular classrooms. This is unusual. Most kids in severely emotionally disturbed programs tend to stay there. Other teachers, working in the same program as Miss Gomez, but not paying attention to moods, did not have the same remarkable results.

Miss Gomez added,

This year they cut two aides out of my class and added more kids. Before I worked with moods, I would have quit or worked under tremendous stress. But now, even with more kids and less help, I handle the class easily. It's remarkable.

Miss Gomez turned her teaching around when she:

- Stopped trying to force teaching through negative moods
- Synchronized teaching and learning to positive moods

GETTING HONEST ABOUT PSYCHOLOGICAL IMPAIRMENT

When we have the flu and feel sick, there's no doubt: we are physically impaired. Not wanting to pass the virus around, knowing we are incapacitated, we postpone activities, take time off until we feel stronger, ready to face responsibilities again. If we have things that must be done, like feeding the children, we use common sense. We don't serve souffle, even if that were what we had planned. Keeping a safe distance, we make do with cereal and toast instead.

This is the same common sense we use when we are suffering from bad-mood virus. We pull back and ease off, taking time-out so we don't start a bad-mood epidemic. In a bad mood, it is not the time, even if it's on the schedule, to:

- Lead 30 kindergartners to a vat of paper mache paste
- Introduce long division
- Ask the principal for money to take the advanced biology class to Hawaii to study tropical flora and fauna
- Give the principal constructive criticism about his tie
- Tell Mrs. Screech she left a mess in the coffee room

If you are a parent, when low mood strikes, do not pick that moment to:

- Tell your spouse there's a better way to load the dishwasher
- Go uninvited into your sloppy kid's room to see if it's clean
- Help your kid with advanced calculus
- Tell your mother to mind her own business

• Talk to your grouchy teenager about anything

If you are a counselor in the throes of mood malaise, this is *not* the time to:

• Yell at your client, "You've got to get your anger under control, you hostile bastard"
• Ask your pacing, screaming, ready-to-explode client, "Is something wrong?"
• Agree with your client that everything is hopeless
• Assess your toughest client's prognosis
• Evaluate your future as a counselor
• Count the years until retirement

THE SECRET

The secret to creating teachable moments is: (1) get yourself in a composed mood; and (2) do what you can to help the other person get in a constructive, hopeful state of mind.

Changed Moment #1: Bill Pulls Himself Together

Bill, in an impatient mood, is grocery shopping with his cranky two-year-old. Bill snaps, "No, for the seventh time, you cannot have a sixteen-ounce bag of Gummy Slimy-Snakes, not now, not tomorrow, not in this lifetime. Forget it." The tot stiffens his body into a board and starts screaming.

This, an unteachable moment, is not the time for reason or lecture. This is a time for acting, for doing whatever is necessary to restore sanity, to get back to a good feeling as soon as possible. The first thing Bill does is get himself under control. Until he does, he won't see solutions. He'll be part of the problem.

Deciding someone has to be the adult, Bill pulls himself together and tries to divert his son's attention by jangling the car keys under his nose. It doesn't work, so he carries his screaming, stiff-as-a-board boy outside to the fresh air. After a few minutes the lad calms down and they go back into the store. Bill gives the youngster a cookie so he can finish shopping in peace. Giving in to common sense, the solution is an easy one and both leave the store happy.

Changed Moment #2: Susan's Kind Action

Susan's eight-year-old daughter, Agatha, is heartbroken. She hugs her mother and cries from such a deep place, Susan would give anything to make her feel better. Susan knows this is not a time for talking but a time for comforting. Susan holds her daughter close. Her kind actions teach more than words could say. This child, with her mother's firm support, will go through grief and come out the other side in an amazingly short period. Later, Susan can be available to answer Agatha's questions if she has any. Some of the most powerful teaching takes place in silence.

Changed Moments #3 and #4: We're Always Teaching

We're always teaching, even when we don't realize it. Sitting in a movie theater waiting for the show to start, Susie was tense, afraid someone tall would sit in front of her and block the screen. Just then, a line of people filed in front of her. One lady had such a serene expression on her face, Susie suddenly realized that she'd lost her own peace of mind; and in that moment's realization, it was back again. The serene lady had no idea she'd created such a beautifully teachable moment.

One day at work, Gloria was so serious, so intent, so goal-oriented that she didn't stop to eat. She didn't notice what state she was in until she literally ran into Jeff in the hallway. He stopped, looked at Gloria with a compassionate smile on his face and said, "Oops. Woman on a mission." Jeff's kindly, humorous, nonjudgmental observation created a teachable moment in which Gloria realized she'd gotten caught up in low-mood thinking without realizing it and was able to back off, relax and return to work in a more composed state of mind.

Ironically, if Gloria's supervisor had called her into his office and said in serious tones, "Gloria, your mood is low. It's bringing other people down and I want you to stop it," Gloria would have argued, justified her position and left the encounter feeling more intense than before. Jeff's spontaneous, good-mood interaction preserved Gloria's dignity, touched her heart and opened her mind.

Changed Moment #5: Dignity Preserved

Upset, feeling more than a shade mean, Janie approaches her husband and in her softest, most practiced, honey-coated tones, she says,

> Honey, don't take this wrong, but an emotionally mature, responsible person doesn't leave his dirty socks all over the house for someone else to pick up. If you really loved me, if you were really sensitive to my needs, you'd know this without my having to bring it up.

Janie's husband, just backsided from his blind spot, is *not* going to say,

> Darling, you are absolutely right. What an inconsiderate, selfish blockhead I've been. Thank you so much for drawing this significant personal weakness to my attention. I'll be a better person from now on, thanks to you. How did I, seriously flawed as I am, ever deserve a truly wonderful woman like you?

Not in your dreams. Janie, trying to disguise her bad-mood, judgmental, I'm-going-to-nail-you-to-the-wall-and-enjoy-it feelings in muted tones, has unknowingly created an *un*teachable moment. Her husband responds to her feeling, *not to her message.* Doing what a person usually does when they feel attacked, he retorts, "Oh, yeah! What about the stockings soaking in my sink every other night? What about your mother. . . ?"

To avoid such tacky, demeaning *un*teachable moments with your loved ones, don't try to convey important messages when you're feeling prickly and can't resist going for the jugular vein. It won't work. People see right through low-mood words and they respond to the feeling. If you're feeling too unhappy to be kind or too sniveling to be honest, wait until you shift into a more comfortable state of mind.

You catch more flies with honey than you do with vinegar. In a positive state of mind, Janie can say anything because her affection will make her words, even strong ones, palatable. In a tender state of mind, Allison can say, "Honey, when I pick up your socks, I want to give away all your clothes, run away from home and leave no forwarding address. Please, honey, if you want to save this marriage, pick up your damn clothes." The message is given and received, everyone's dignity is preserved, no one feels bruised, rejected or like a bad person and the healthy family feeling is preserved.

Changed Moment #6: Finding a Compassionate Feeling

A teacher, after asking his students to read two poems, asked students which one they liked best. Bette, age twelve, took her time to answer. The teacher said: "I was hoping you'd answer sometime before the end of the semester. Make up your mind, if you have one." Bette blushed while her classmates giggled.

Mockery, sarcasm, making jokes at someone's expense does not open people's minds. To teach rather than ridicule, this teacher could have found a compassionate feeling and said, "I know it's not easy to decide. Parts of both poems are appealing. Which one speaks most to your heart?"

Communicating in a Negative Mood

How do you communicate responsibly when you're in a lousy mood? Usually, you can act a little nicer than you feel, but not much, so you proceed carefully, thoughtfully, humbly, like driving on ice.

1. Tell how you feel.
2. Take responsibility for your feelings, giving "I" messages instead of "*you*" messages.

3. Stay in the present (don't drag in the past, too!)
4. Be brief, to the point.

For example:

I'm in a stinking mood. I have murder on my mind. It's all I can do to keep myself under control. If pressed, I cannot be responsible for what I might say or do. Don't touch me. Don't talk to me. Don't look at me. I'll get back to you later.

Or:

I'm so upset I can't talk to you now. I don't trust what I will say or do. Go to your room and we'll talk later, after I've calmed down.

Or:

Yes, something is definitely wrong but trust me, you don't want to know what it is right now. I'm going for a walk to pull myself together. We'll talk later when my mind is clear.

Or:

Don't tell me now. I can't listen. I'm worried and I can't think clear. Please be patient.

Or:

When you interrupt me in the middle of a sentence, I feel like you don't care enough about me to listen.

These "I" messages are honest, responsible, teachable communication. Compare and contrast them to these examples of *un*teachable moments.

I'm miserable and it's all your fault. Because of you, I'm giving away my bird, selling my house and moving away. If you were an intelligent, responsible, loving, sensitive person, you would never have done what you did. How could you?

Or:

I know why you did that. You did that because you are mean, selfish, lazy and irresponsible. I see right through you. Don't try to lie out of it and don't play dumb. Everybody sees it, everyone's talking about it.

Or:

What's wrong with you? Don't you ever think? Don't you know *anything*? Why must you *always* . . . Why is it you *never* . . .

Or:

If you don't stop that I'm going to kick your butt.

A rule of thumb is, if you must communicate in sour moods, talk about yourself, not what you will do. Resist the almost overwhelming temptation to tell others what's wrong with them, what terrible things you think they are thinking, what dastardly motivation you think is behind their behavior. Everyone thinks differently than everyone else. Just because you are thinking something, that does not mean other people are thinking it too. What other people are actually thinking usually comes as a complete surprise.

The key to communication in a bad mood is to do as little damage as possible while you await the return of your sanity.

WAYS CLASSROOM TEACHERS CHANGE MOODS

Every teacher needs to have standby options, things to do when bad-mood attacks. Here are some things other teachers do to create the space where good-mood can happen.

- Show a film, video.
- Assign high-interest, easy-to-do seat work.
- Go for a ten minute nature walk.
- Start a lively discussion about something you're really interested in.
- Change the activity. Do something you enjoy.

To Help Students Change from Agitated to Composed States of Mind:

Sometimes the teacher's mood is fine but the collective classroom mood is unteachable. Teachers also need standby activities that provide the mental distraction that will bring a mood shift in youngsters. Here are some tried and true oldies but goodies.

- Read aloud a story or poem.
- Sing a song, whistle a tune, play the harmonica.
- Play Twenty Questions or some other game.
- Tell jokes, ask a riddle, pose a brain-teaser.
- Do a trick and see if the students can figure out how it's done.
- Pass out treats.
- Take an exercise break.
- Have a period of silence or soothing music, a relaxation break.
- Do the unexpected. Put on Groucho glasses, pull out a puppet, a wind up toy or a silly hat.
- Have five minutes of free time.

Be creative. Freshen things up. The point is to break the bad-mood habit and find the feelings that make teaching and learning a joy.

SUMMARY

Unteachable moments are a fact of life. Every teacher, parent and counselor has to be adept at changing unteachable moments to teachable ones. Fortunately, it's not difficult to do. The most difficult part is learning to recognize when a moment is unteachable and then being willing to step back and take the time to create a turning point. To create turning points, to go from unteachable to teachable, use your creativity and common sense. It's fun. And you won't believe what a difference it will make.

17 | Realizing a Higher Level of Consciousness

Teaching is a precious work.

Teachers impact the future, leaving their stamp, not only on today, but on tomorrow as well. Teachers want to make things better for people. But we can't make things better for others until we make them better for ourselves. We can't teach what we don't know. We can't give what we don't have. To institute a new era of teaching and learning effectiveness, we must first institute a new level of consciousness.

When our current teaching practices were formulated, knowledge about thought and how it works was, for all practical purposes, nonexistent. Not understanding thought, we based our teaching practices on theories that did not consider that perception, motivation, discouragement, frustration, stress, disability, failure and dysfunctional behavior are all outgrowths of the thinking process.

A revolution in teaching requires a new understanding of what thinking is. It takes courage to examine our old beliefs and realize they are what's been holding us back. They are what's been contaminating our results and interfering with our dreams.

Now we have, for the first time, the psychological understanding to create first-rate, break-the-mold teachable and learnable moments for ourselves and others. Now we know:

- *Besides the intelligence correlated with IQ, every person has a deeper, innate level of consciousness, called wisdom or common sense.*

- *In discouraged, frustrated or insecure states of mind, thought is separated from this deeper level of creative consciousness and potential is restricted.*

- *In composed, optimistic, secure states of mind, deeper wisdom operates through the experience of insight, freeing potential.*

With these realizations, people who want to help others will make their teaching more humane, joy-filled and compassionate, not just because it's more pleasant, but because the human mind is at its peak of power in positive states and impaired in negative ones. People who want optimal learning will eliminate humiliation and fear of failure from teaching, not just because it doesn't feel good, but because it closes minds and clouds thought. People who want teaching excellence will eliminate stress, strain and tension from their interactions, not just because it's uncomfortable, but because stress is to the mind what overheating is to a fine engine.

For the first time, we have the understanding to choose our level of consciousness. Aware of our role as thinkers, we can choose to be conscious of what's right or what's wrong; what's healthy or what's dysfunctional; what's uplifting or what's depressing; what's ugly or what's beautiful. It's an important choice. Whatever fills our consciousness fills our thoughts. Whatever fills our thoughts is what makes or breaks our students.

When our thoughts are filled with criticism, we teach condemnation. When our thoughts are filled with encouragement, we teach success. When our thoughts are filled with love, we teach self-esteem. When our thoughts are full of hope, we teach well-being.

Excellent teachers and superior learners cannot indulge in low-mood, negative thinking. In insecure states of mind we produce negative thoughts, which we then try to analyze. Lost in negative thought with no awareness that we are the thinker, we get trapped on one level of consciousness and we can't see options. We think more about problems than solutions, more about what doesn't work than what does work, more about what we can't do than what we can do. To create teachable moments, we cannot cater to states of mind that produce discouragement, pessimism, belittling judgments, derogatory assumptions, fault-finding interpretations or demeaning expectations. This is the old way.

If excellence is more than lip-service, we must accept our responsibility as thinkers, quiet our insecurities, elevate our moods, open our minds, forget what we've learned in the past and look for insight to usher in a new level of thought, a new logic of teaching based on wisdom and common sense.

Then we will ensure achievement, productivity and success, not just for a few, but for everyone. Teachers never know where their influence ends. Students come back years later, and say, "You changed my life when you said. . . . " and for the life of you, you don't even remember it! Inevitably, these memorable lessons are of caring, kindness and warmth.

The 1960s and 1970s saw the emergence of a humanistic teaching movement with emphasis on feelings. The 1980s saw a return to back-to-the-basics, which downplayed emotions. Because of our up-dated psychological base, the 1990s will use the best of both worlds where people work in higher levels of consciousness, teaching the basics with new feeling and enjoying unprecedented results.

We can't wait to change. There will always be too much to do. There will never be enough time. There will always be problems, perfectly justifiable reasons to be crabby, peevish, morose, hopeless. But we can't wait. There is too much at stake.

If we are ever going to be more than we are, now is the time to do it. Now is the time to make schools places where people *love* to be; places where learning is fun and full of life; places where everyone, teachers included, is treated with dignity, courtesy and respect; places where everyone belongs and feels valued, competent, lovable; places where the highest wisdom is expressed in patience and kindness; places where, because it's virtually impossible to fail, everyone is inspired to higher achievement by the unequalled feeling of success.

Now is the time to makes homes comfortable, friendly, good-mood places, places of sharing, laughter and fun, safe places of generosity, affection and acceptance, restful places where people can let down their guard and be themselves, where they can relax from the day's work and fill up for tomorrow's challenges.

Imagine counseling offices where people learn to use their thinking to produce mental health rather than mental distress; places where people learn to use their thinking to help them relax instead of producing tension, places where people learn to rise above insecure thought to discover the lighter, more loving, beautiful side of life; places where clients leave sessions feeling more connected, stronger, more happy and hopeful than when they came in.

To achieve higher levels of consciousness, it's time to throw chronic seriousness, insecurity and self-consciousness to the wind. It is time to forego gnashing, gnarling, forcing, pushing, and straining. If these things were going to make us excellent teachers and learners, they'd have done it long ago.

Other people, circumstances and situations don't have to change before we can create teachable moments. Our thoughts about people, circumstances and situations must change. Before change can come in the front door, negative thinking has to go out the back door.

"We are on the brink of something that is as beautiful as it is unthinkable. We are on the brink of finding out what happens when a society begins to discover that common sense, wisdom, love, understanding, compassion, and so forth are words that describe the same thing, *mental health*."[1]

To find a new level of consciousness, open your mind to insight. Practice the gentle arts of interest, fascination, delight, and humor. Smile for no reason. Laugh out loud. Play. Be funny. Rekindle the adventurous, energetic loving-to-learn attitude you had as a child. Fall in love again, with yourself, your family, your work, your city, your planet.

Love is more than a pleasurable feeling. It is who we are, the heart of us, the keeps-us-going feeling that we are growing, changing, moving toward something good; the key to creating shining, teachable moments that make things better for people.

NOTES

Chapter 1. What are Teachable Moments?

1. Suarez, Rick, Roger C. Mills and Darlene Stewart. 1987. *Sanity, Insanity and Common Sense*. New York: Fawcett Columbine.

Chapter 3. Putting Teachable Moments to the Test

1. *Gates-MacGinitie Reading Tests*. 1926-78. Walter H. MacGinitie (test and manual) Joyce Kamons, Ruth L. Kowalski, Ruth K. MacGinitie, Timothy MacKay (manual) Riverside Publishing Company.

Chapter 4. Intelligence Beyond IQ

1. Spearman, Charles. 1904. "General intelligence" objectively determined and measured. *American Journal of Psychology* 52, pp. 296-305.

2. Maslow, Abraham. 1968. *Toward A Psychology of Being*. (2nd ed.) New York: Van Nostrand Reinhold.

3. Rogers, Carl. 1942. *Counseling and Psychotherapy*. Boston: Houghton Mifflin.

Chapter 5. Wisdom in Action

1. Axline, Virginia. 1947. *Play Therapy*. New York. Ballantine Books.

2. Moustakas, Clark. 1959. Psychotherapy With Children. *The Living Relationship*. New York: Ballantine.

3. Rogers, Carl. 1961. *On Becoming a Person; A Therapist's View of Therapy*. Boston: Houghton Mifflin.

Chapter 6. Two Dimensions of Thought

1. Pascal. *Pensees*. 1670. p. 347.

Chapter 8. Unrecognized Beliefs Can Cripple Your Potential

1. Rosenthal, R. and L. Jacobson. 1968. *Pygmalion in The Classroom*. New York: Holt, Rinehart and Winston.
2. Page, E.B. 1958. Teacher comments and student performance; A seventy-four classroom experiment in school motivation. *Journal of Educational Psychology*. 49, 173-181.
3. Good, T.L. and J.E. Brophy. 1973. *Looking in Classrooms*. New York: Harper and Row.
4. Matthews, Jay. 1988. *Escalante: The Best Teacher In America*. New York: Henry Holt and Company, Inc.

Chapter 10. Insight: The Heart of the Moment

1. Piaget, Jean. 1973. *The psychology of intelligence*. Totowa, N.J.: Littlefield, Adams.
2. Erikson, E.H. 1963. *Childhood and society*. New York: Horton.
3. Kohlberg, L. 1969. The cognitive-developmental approach to socialization. In *Handbook of socialization theory and research*. ed. D.A. Goslin, pp. 347-380, Chicago: Rand McNalley.
4. Skinner, B.F. 1953. *Science and Human Behavior*. New York: Macmillan.
5. Keller, Helen. 1980. *The Story of My Life*. Mahwah, N.J.: Watermill Press. p. 23-24.
6. James, William. 1982. *Varieties of Religious Experience*. New York: Penguin Classics.
7. Barron, Frank. 1963. *Creativity and Psychological Health*. Princeton: D. Van Nostrand; Drevdahl, John E., and Raymond B. Cattrell. 1958. Personality and creativity in artists and writers. *Journal of Clinical Psychology* 14, pp. 107-111; Rees, M., and M. Goldman. 1961. Some relationships between creativity and personality. *Journal of General Psychology* 65, pp. 145-161;

Wallach, M.A., and N. Kogan. 1965. *Modes of Thinking in Young Children*. New York: Holt, Rinehart & Winston; Giovacchini, Peter L. 1960. On scientific creativity. *Journal of the American Psychoanalytic Association* 8, pp. 407-426; Levy, N.J. 1961. Notes on the creative process and the creative person. *Psychiatric Quarterly* 35, pp 66-77; Maslow, Abraham H. 1958. Emotional blocks to creativity. *Journal of Individual Psychology* 14, pp. 51-56; Rogers, Carl R. 1954. Toward a theory of creativity. ETC: *Review of General Semantics* 11, pp. 249-260.

8. Adamson, R.E. and D.W. Taylor. 1954. Functional fixedness as related to elapsed time and set. *Journal of Experimental Psychology* 47, pp. 122-216; Parnes, S.J. and A. Meadow. 1959. Effects of "brainstorming" instructions on creative problem-solving by trained and untrained subjects. *Journal of Educational Psychology* 50, pp. 171-176; Parnes. S.J. 1961. Effects of extended effort in creative problem-solving. *Journal of Educational Psychology* 52, pp. 117-122.

9. Osborn, Alex F. 1957. *Applied Imagination*. New York: Charles Scribner's Sons; Higgins, J. 1967. Creativity in comic strip authors. *Journal of Creative Behavior* 1, pp. 366-369; Gavin, I.A. 1969. The generation of humorous responses by creative and non-creative college freshmen. Unpublished. Boston State College.

Chapter 13. How Moods Affect Your Performance

1. Csizszentmihalyi, Mihaly. 1990. *Flow, The Psychology of Optimal Experiences*. New York: Harper and Row.

Chapter 15. Changing Moods: Psychological First Aid

1. Friedan, Betty. 1963. *Feminine Mystique*. New York: Dell Publishing Co., Inc.

2. Beattie, Melody. 1989. *Beyond Codependency: And Getting Better All the Time*. New York: Harper and Row.

Chapter 17. Realizing a Higher Level of Consciousness

1. Suarez, *et.al.* 1987. pp. 272-273.

INDEX

About the Author

Darlene Stewart, M.S., a licensed mental health counselor, has over 30 years experience in the fields of education and counseling psychology. She has worked as a classroom teacher, school counselor, mental health counselor, teacher trainer and educational consultant. She is coauthor of the book, *Sanity, Insanity and Common Sense*.